Love is a choice love is something we choose

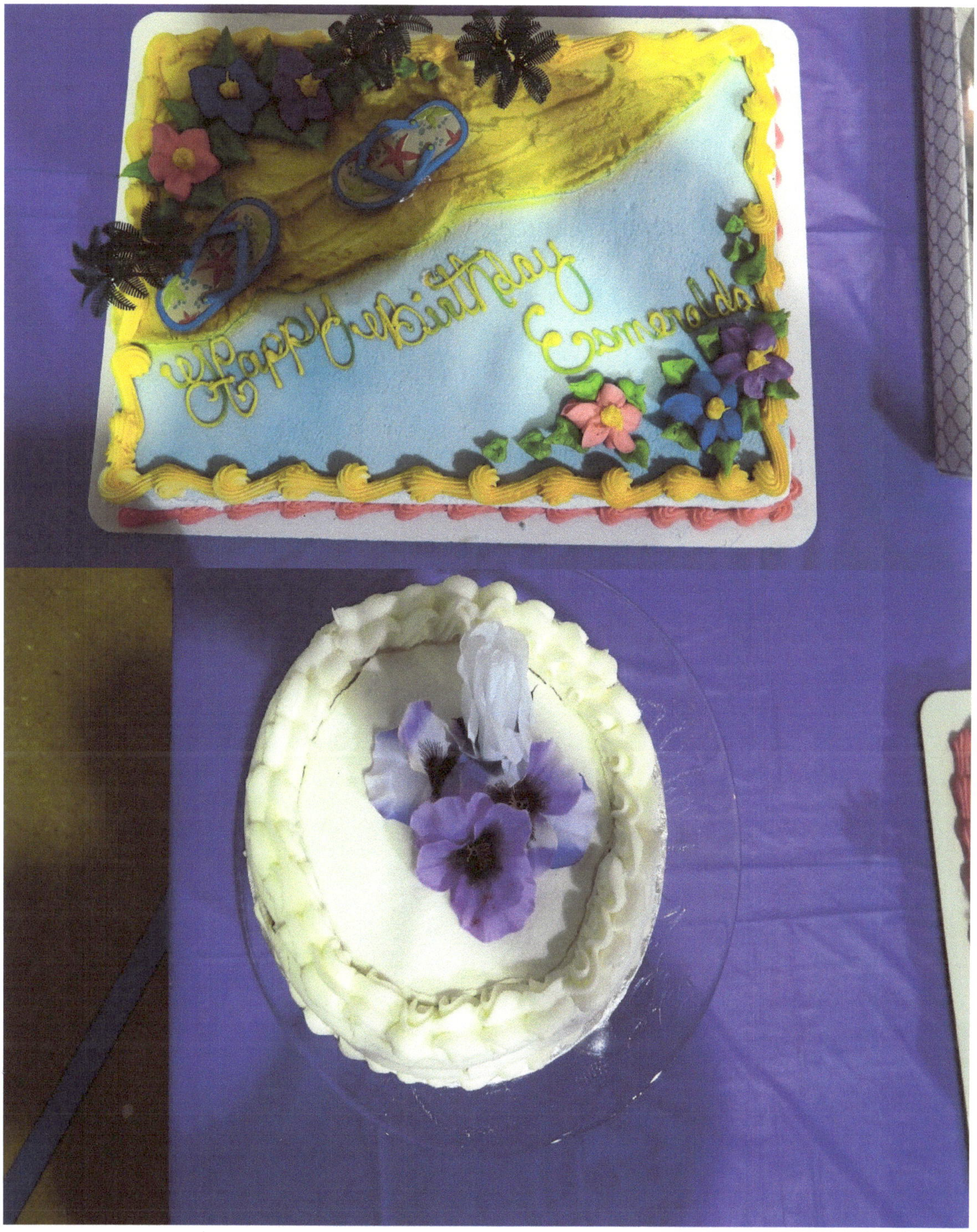

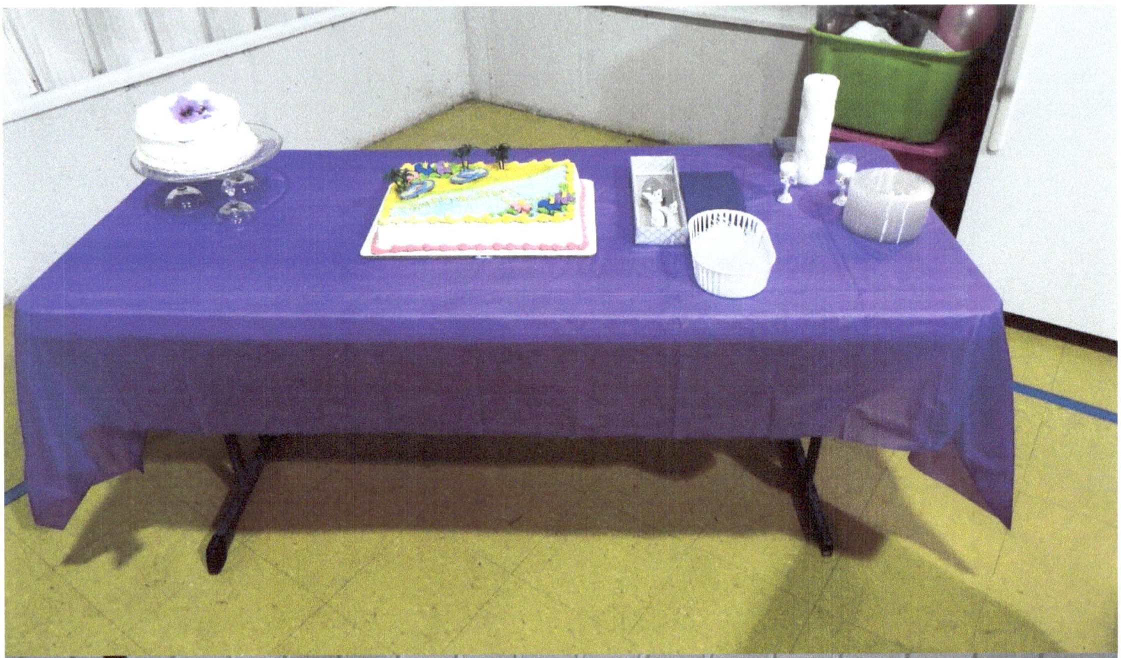

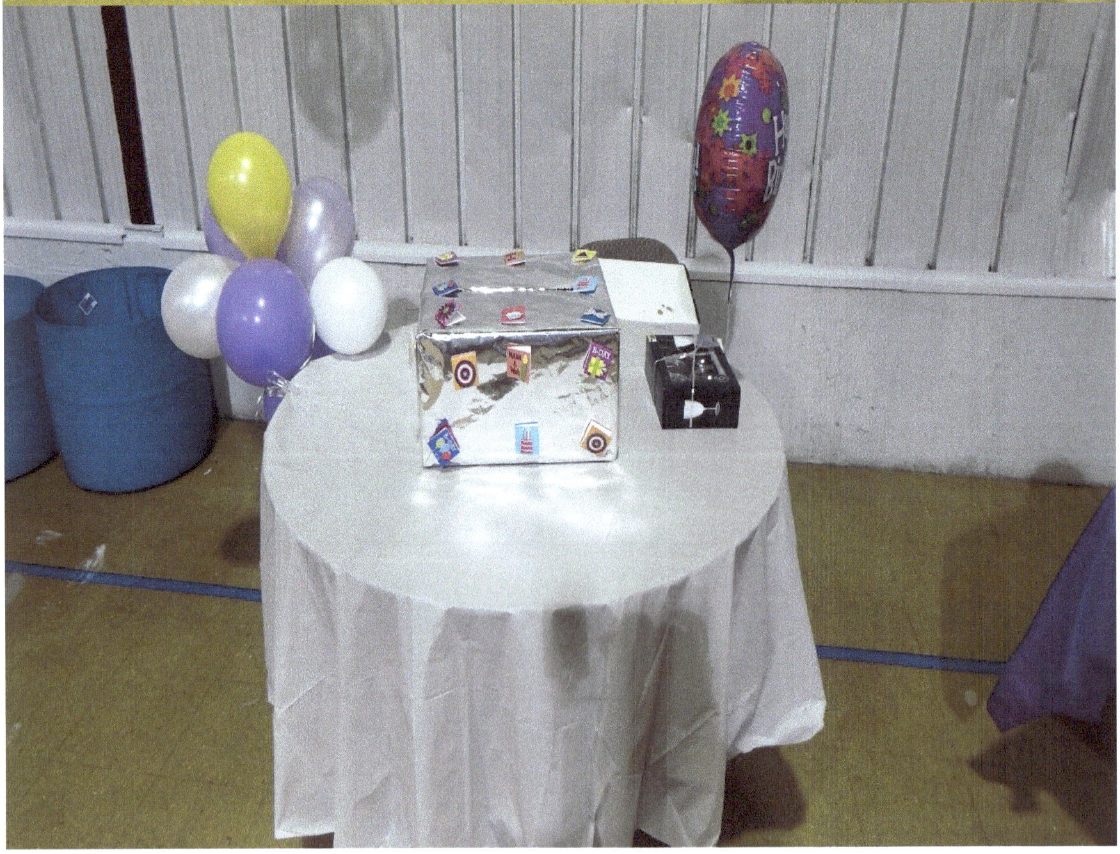

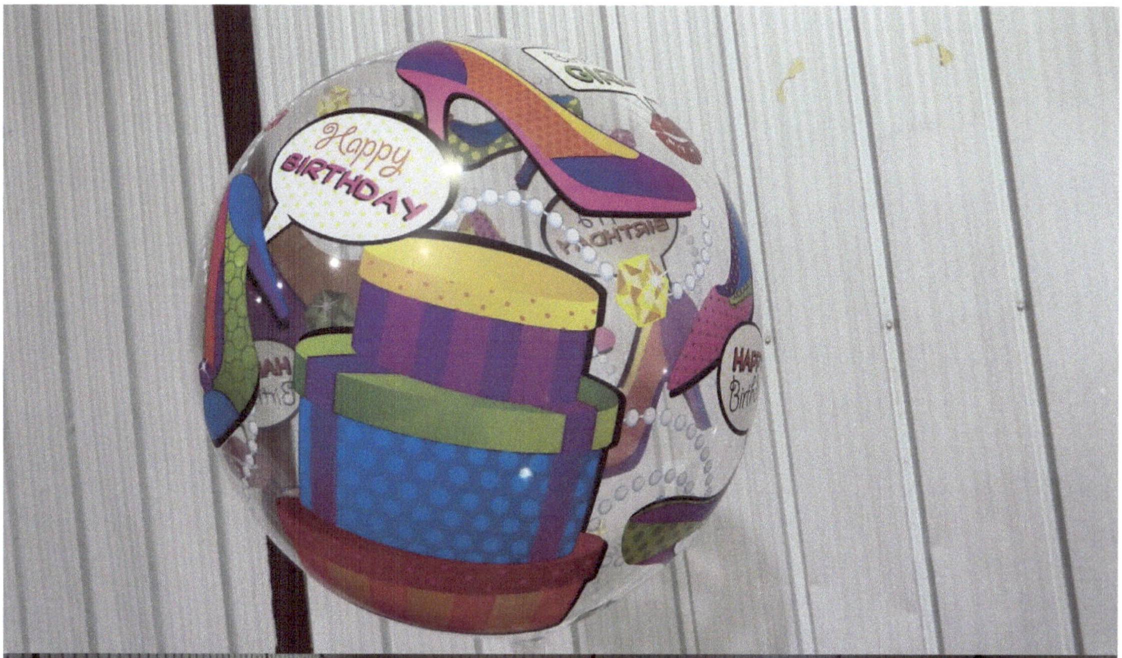
Happy BIRTHDAY
HAPPY

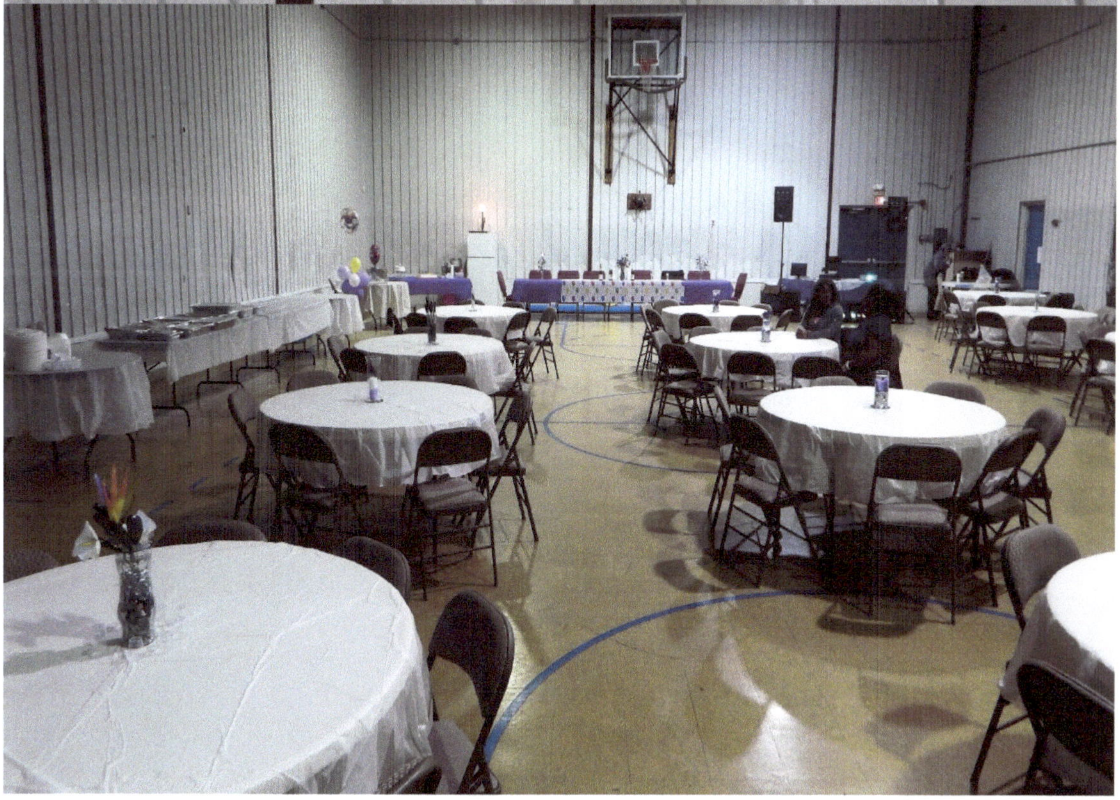

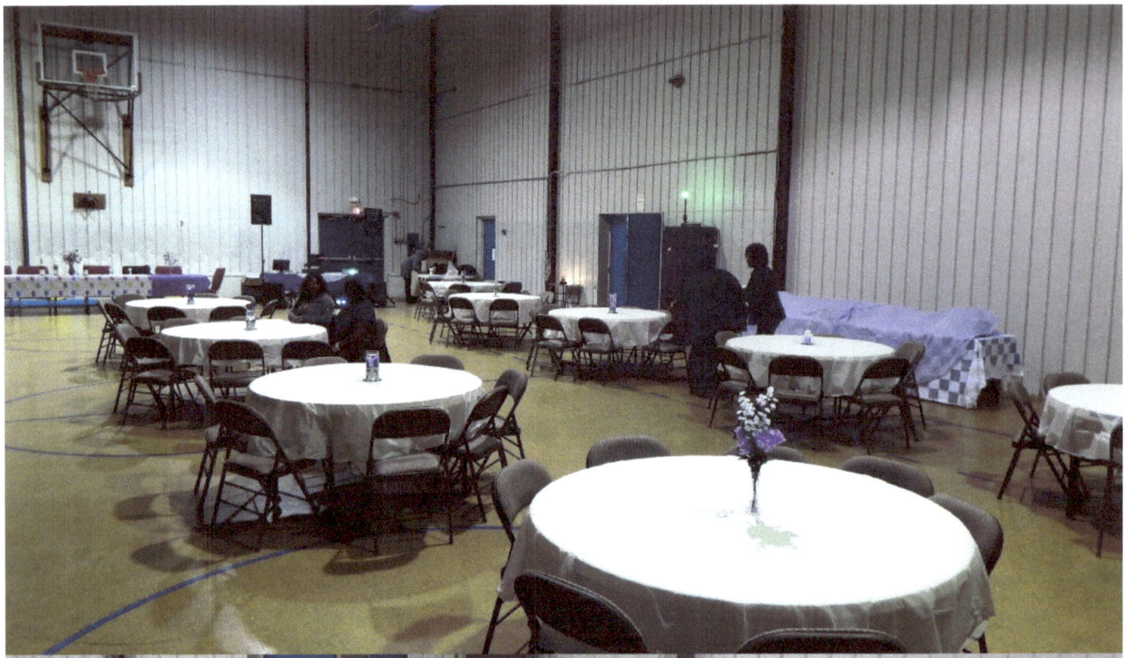

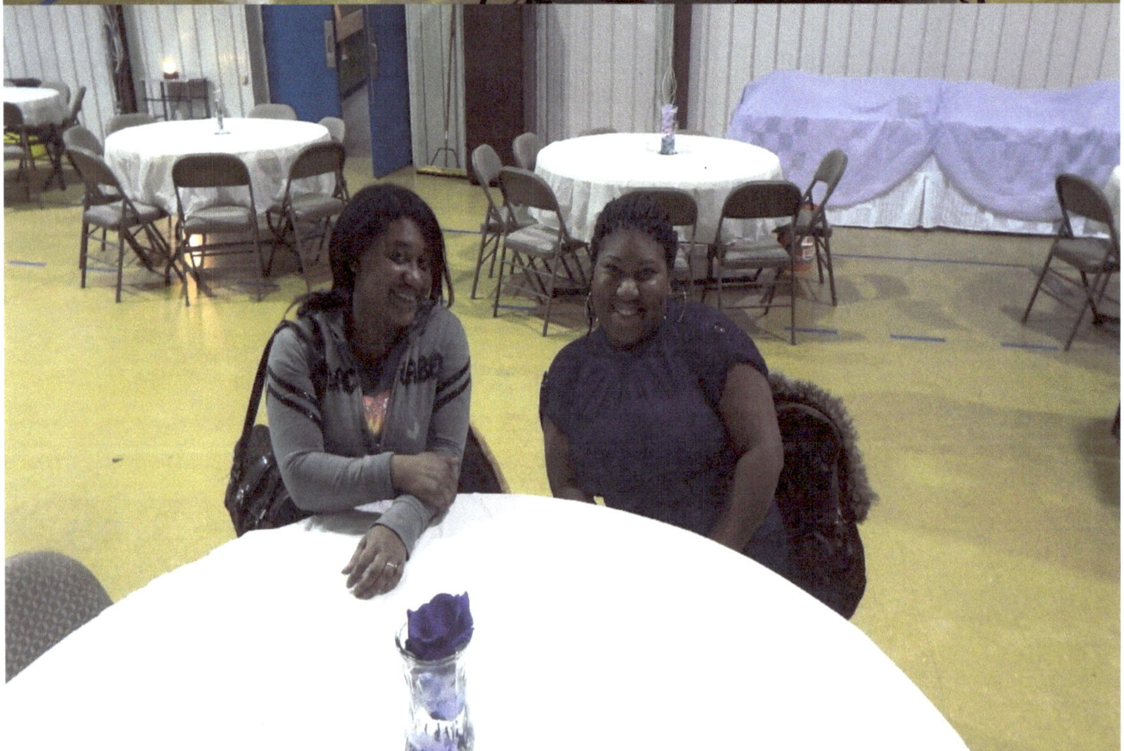

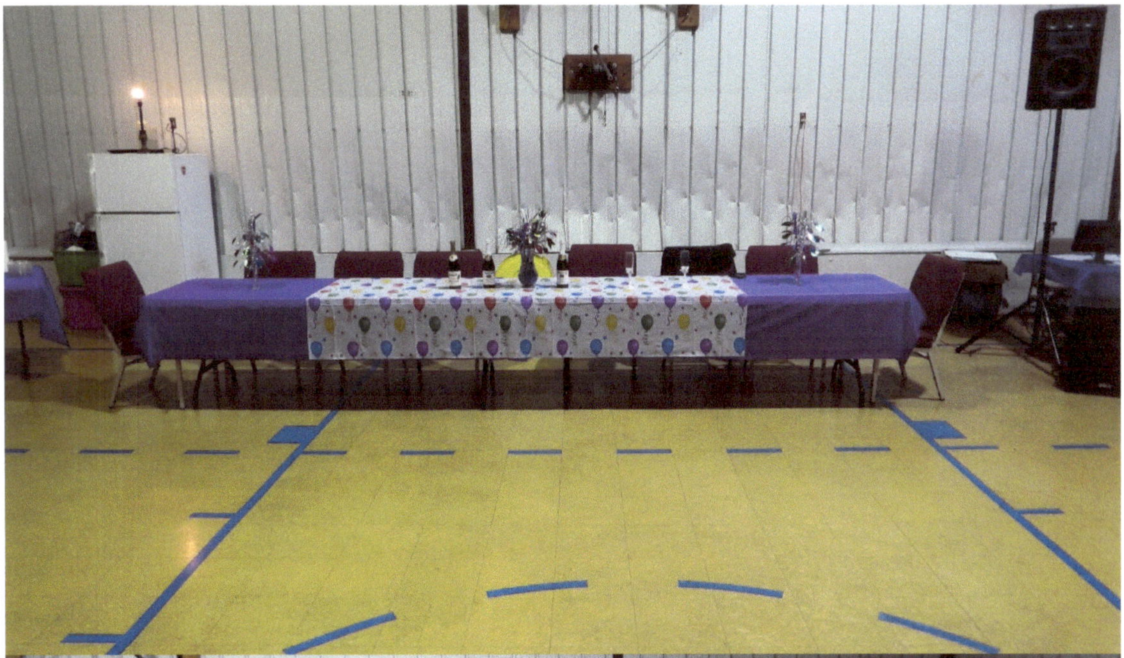

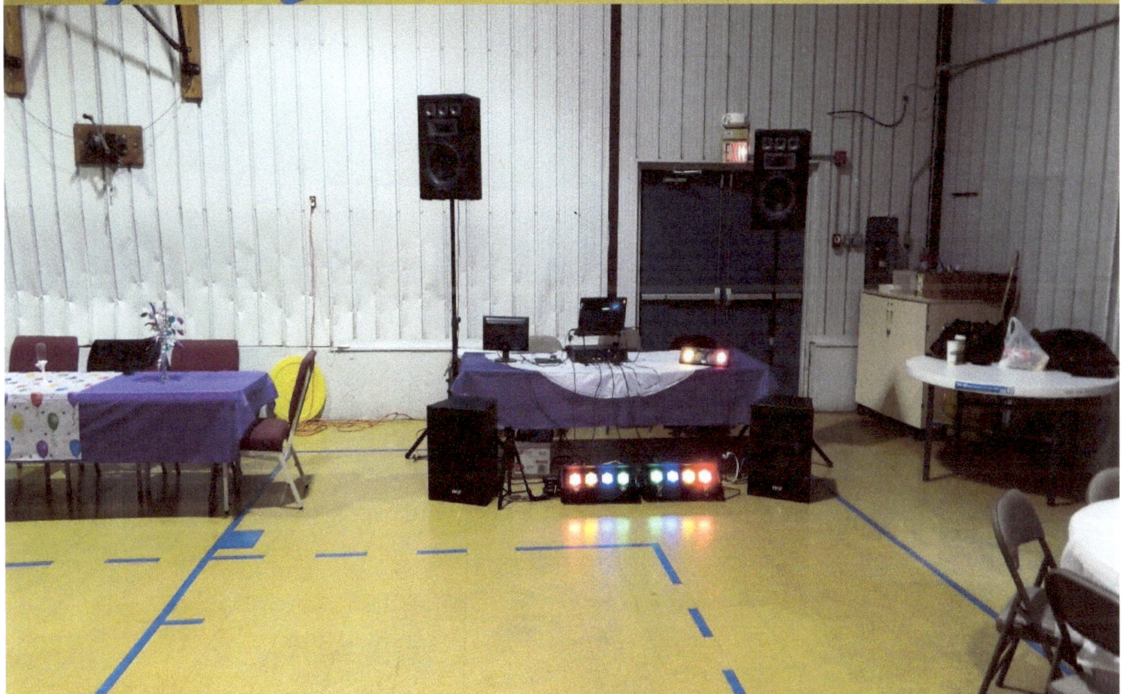

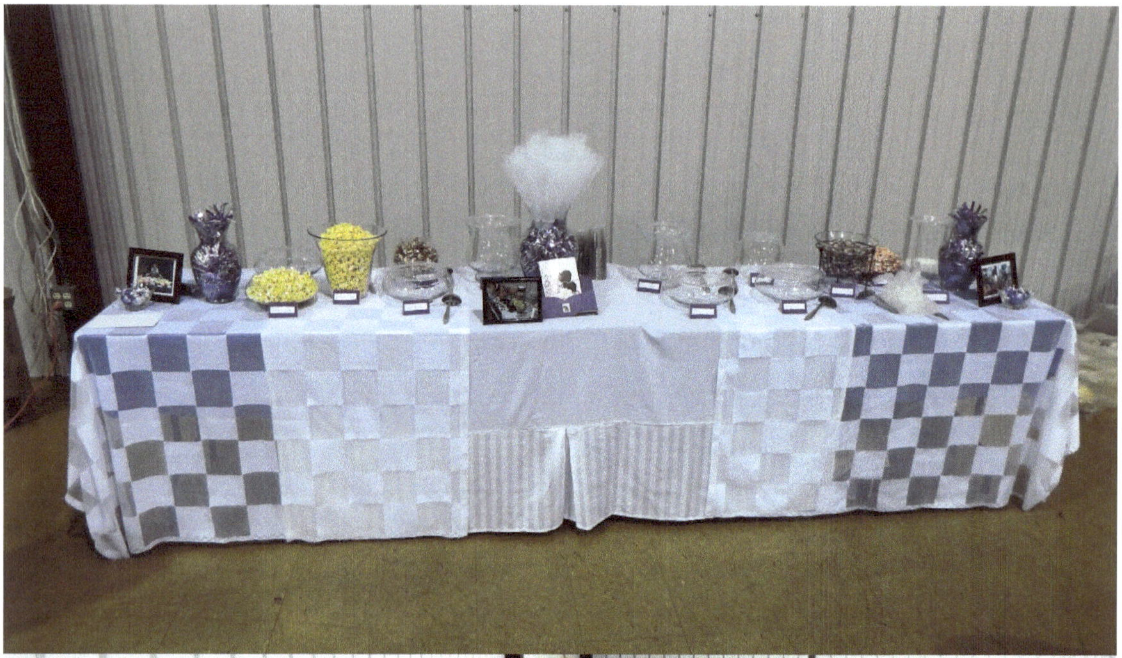

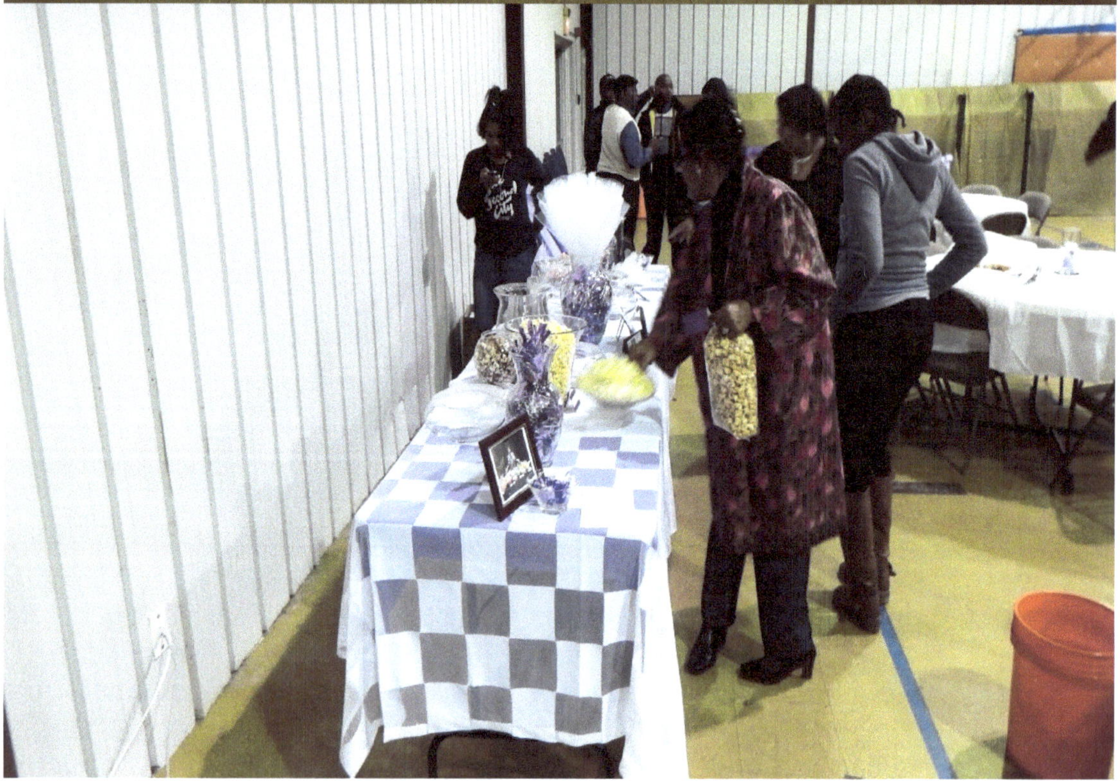

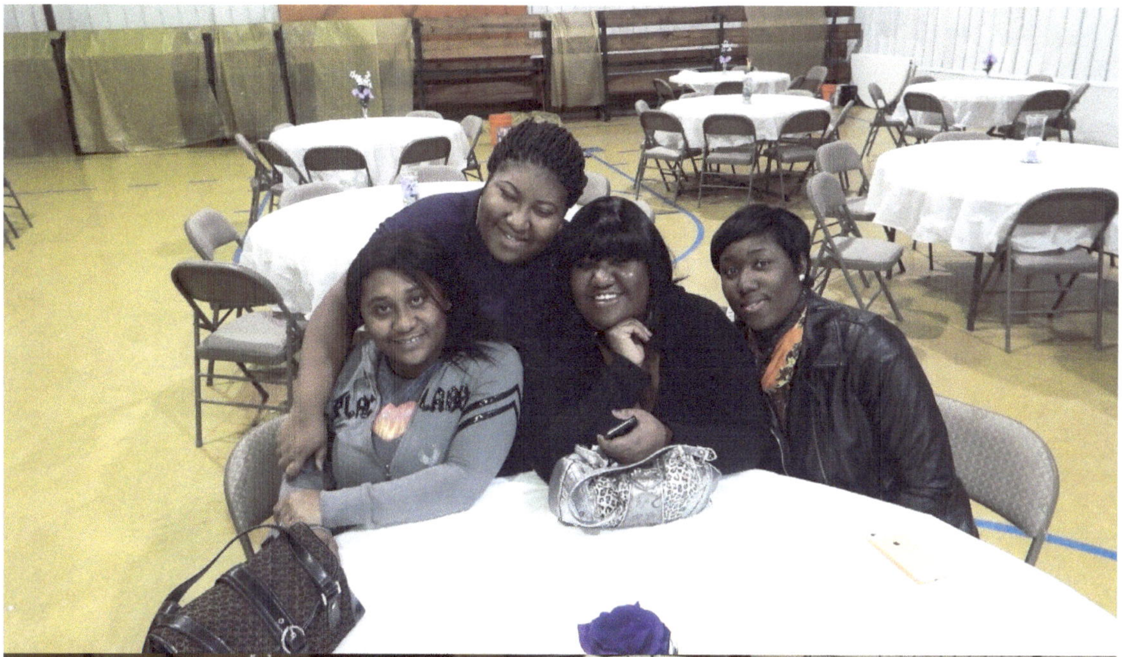

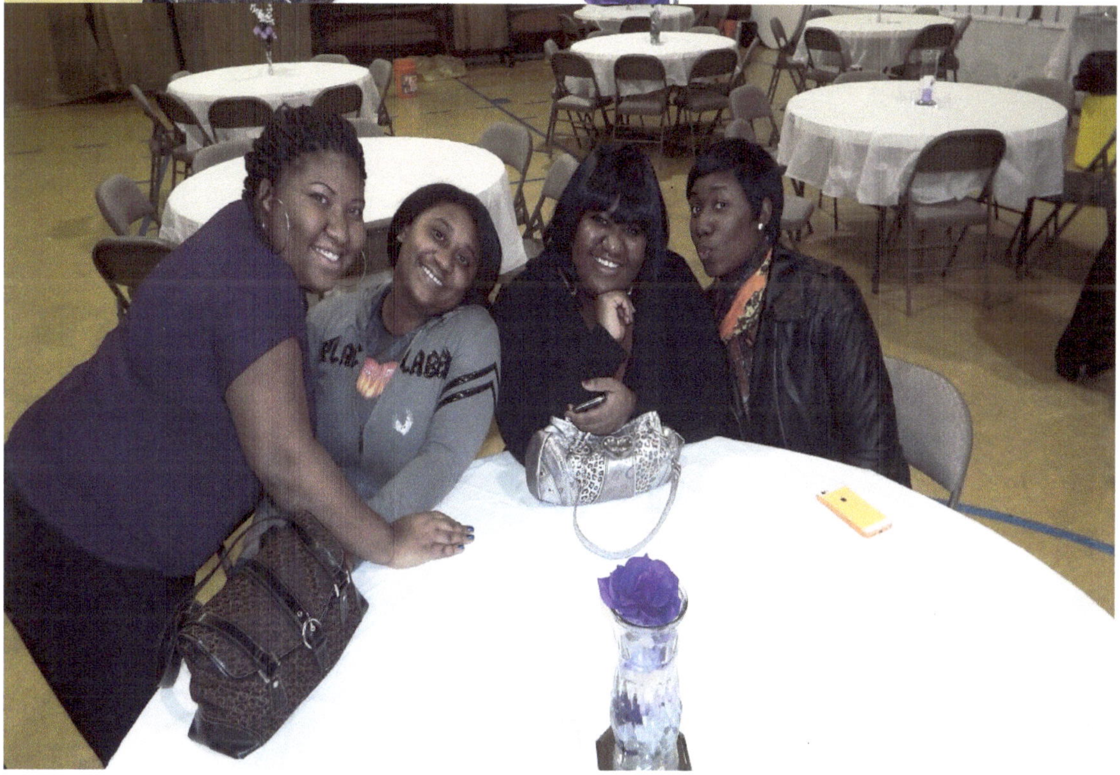

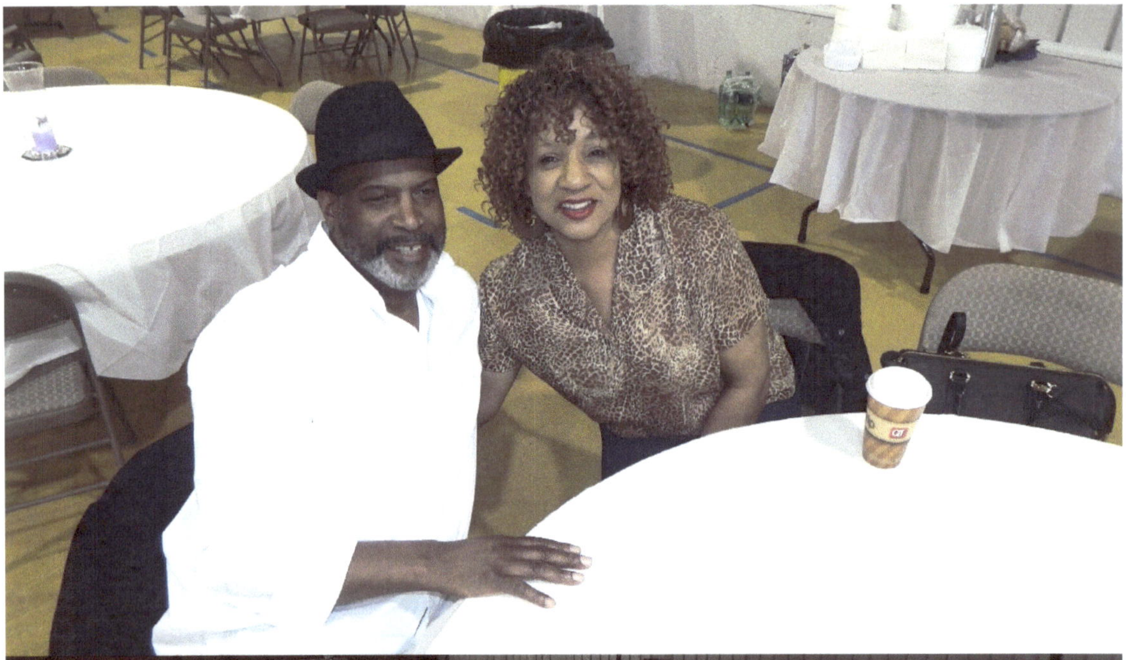

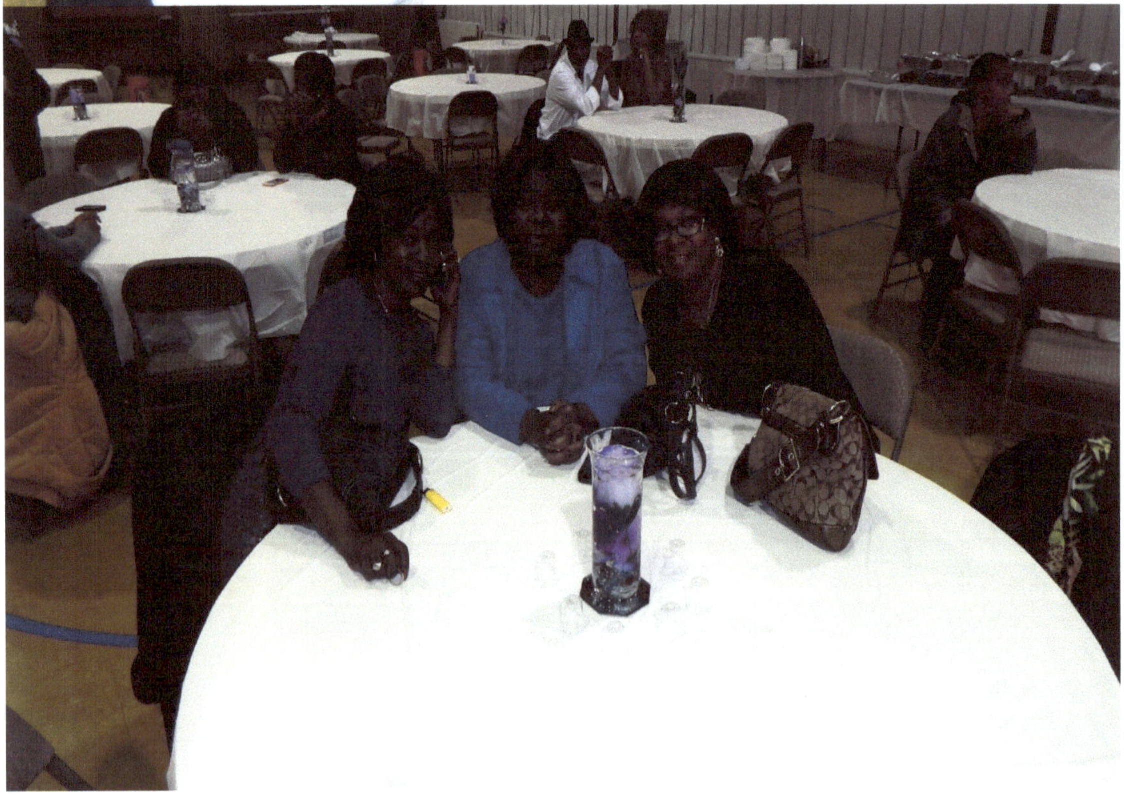

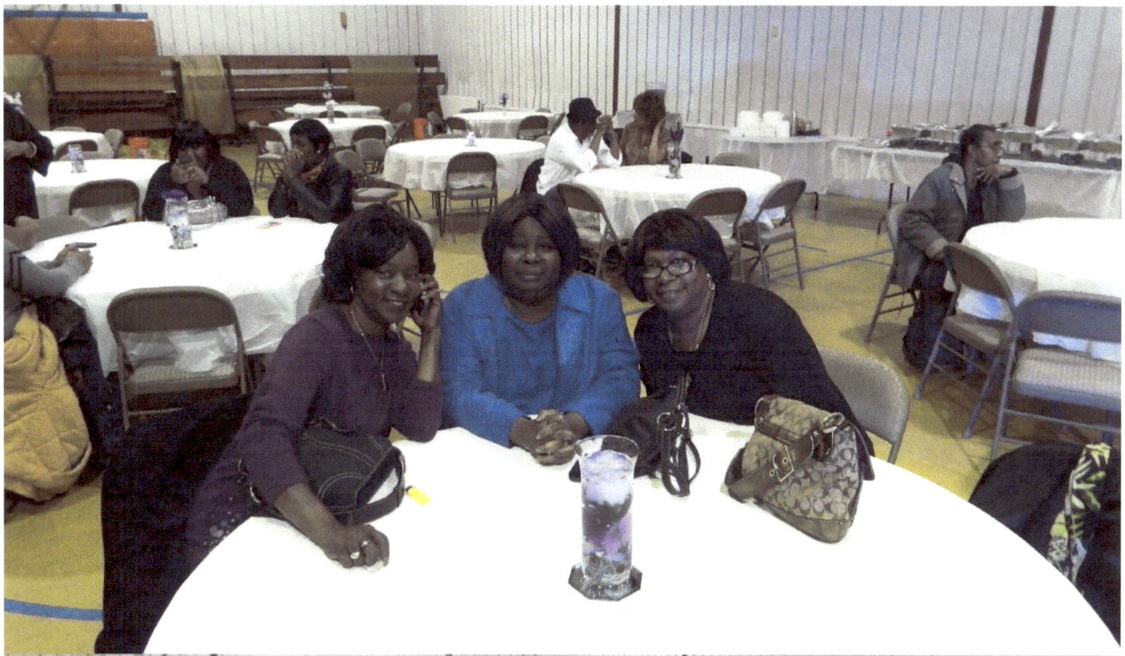

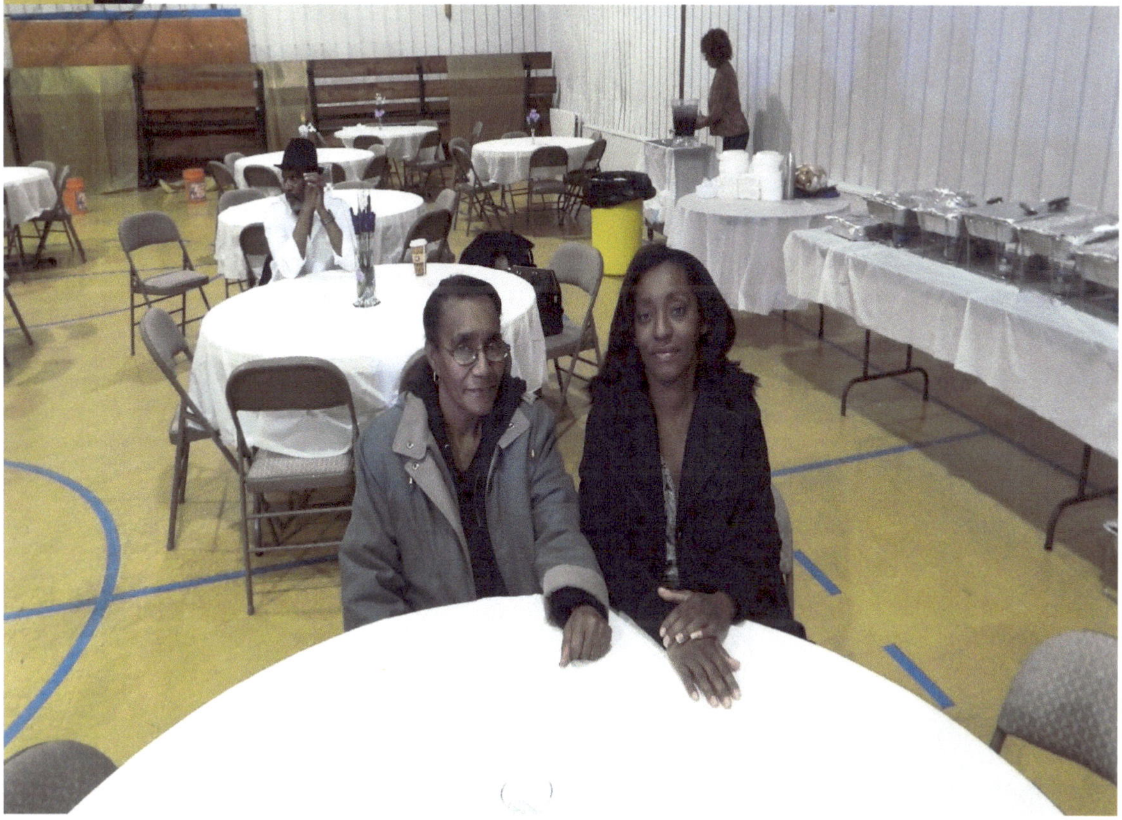

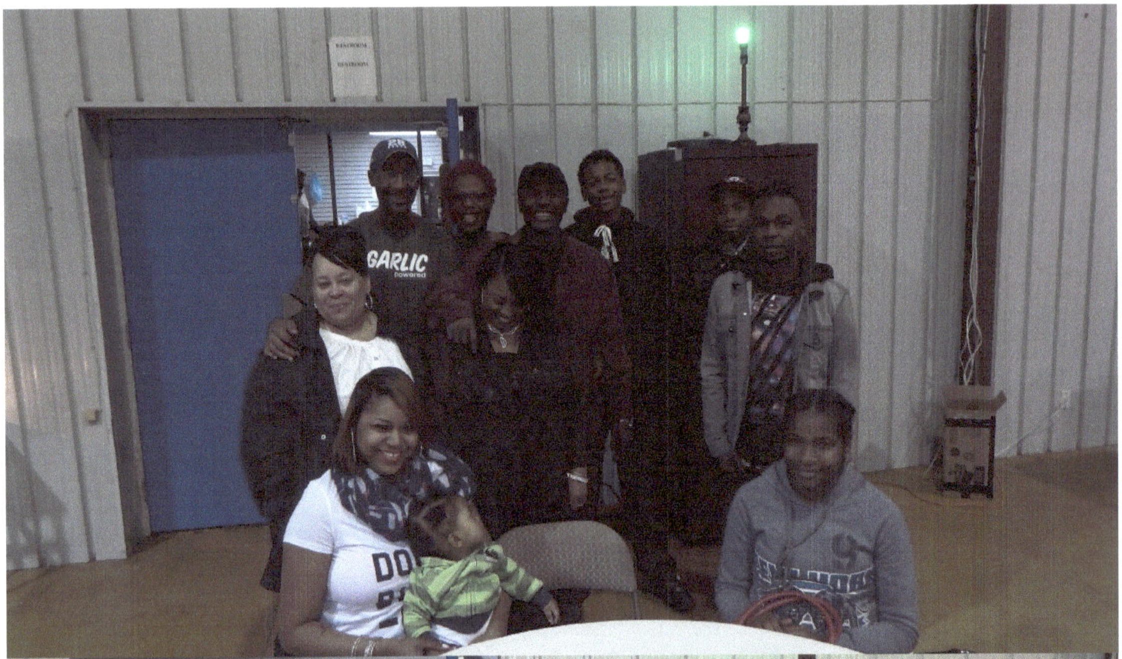
GARLIC
powered

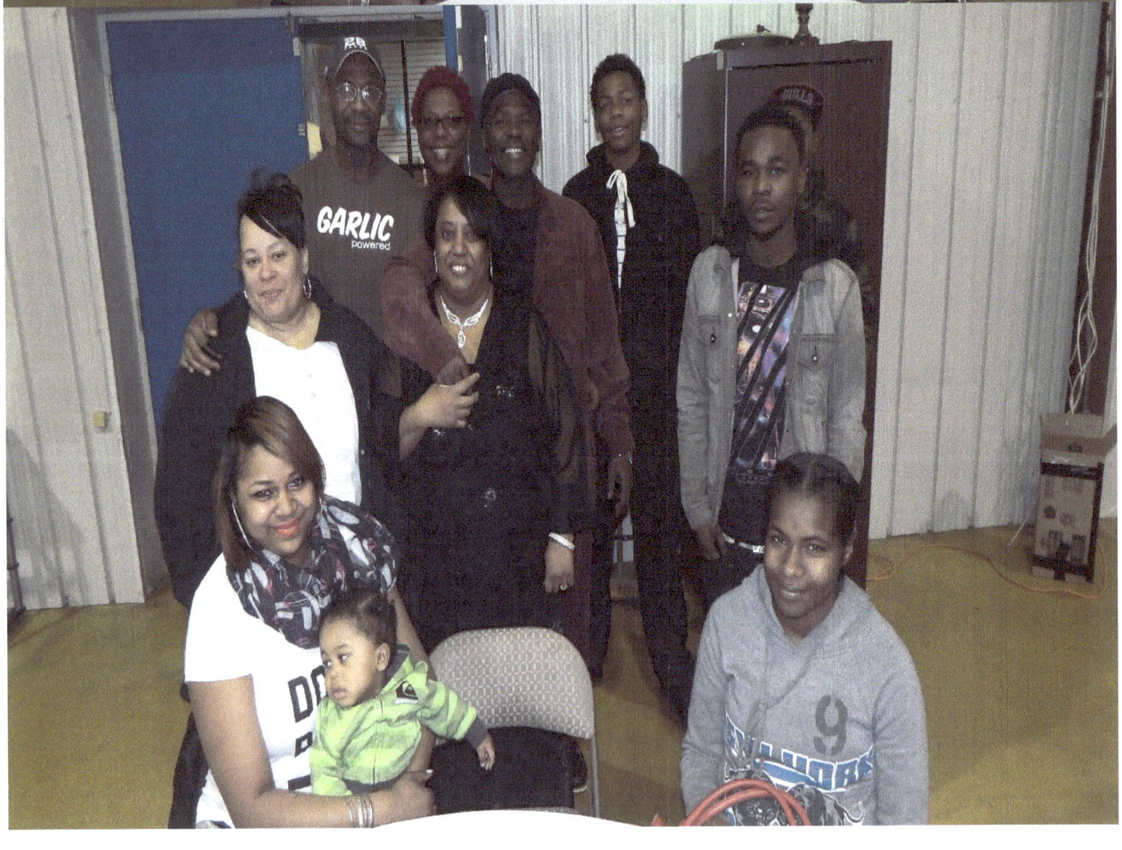
GARLIC
powered

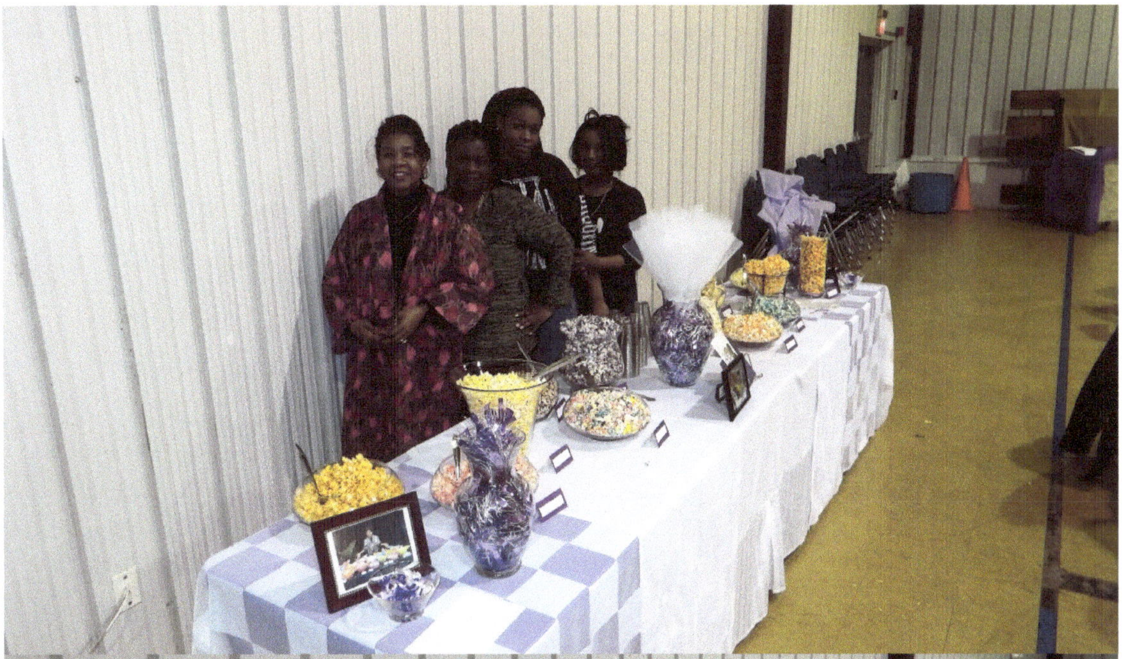

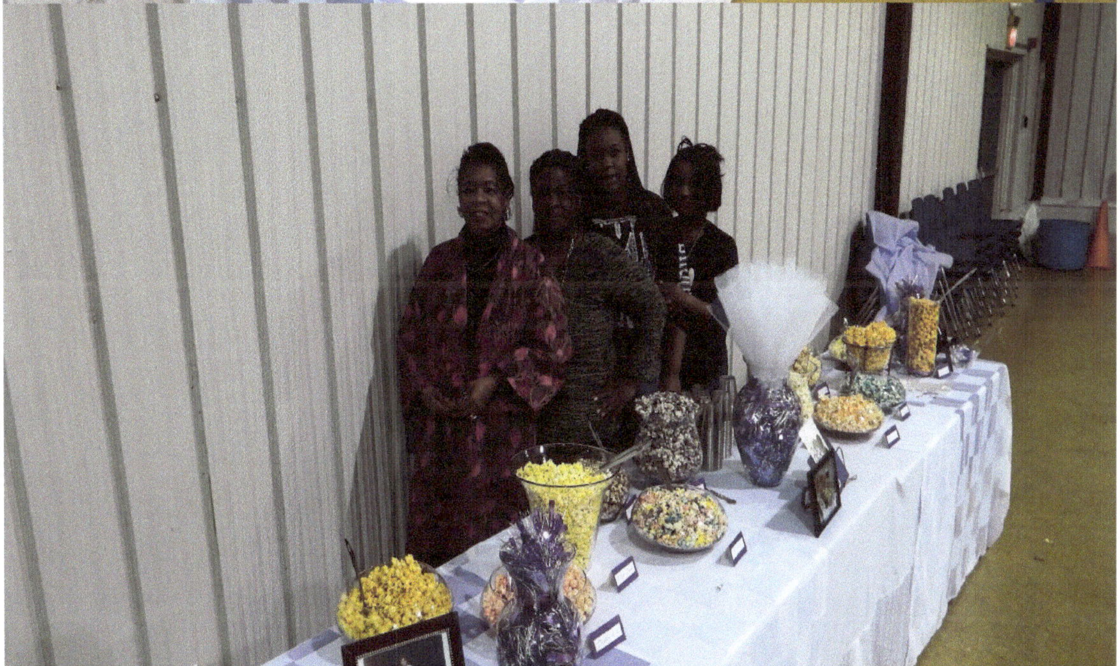

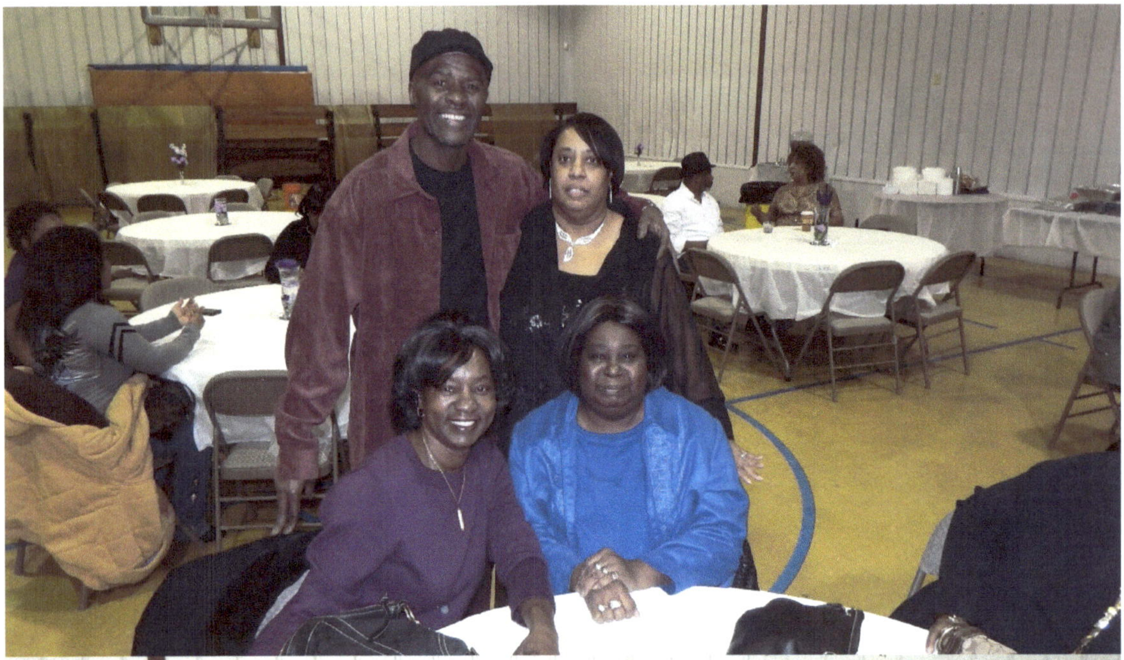

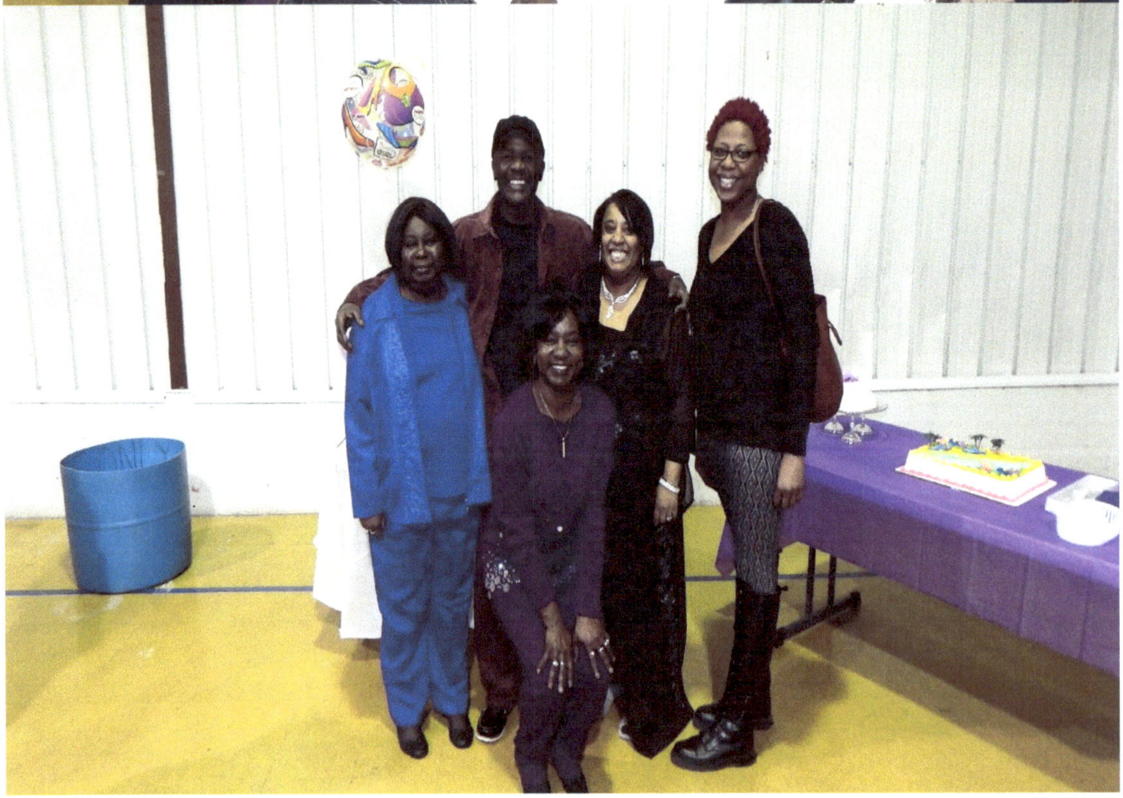

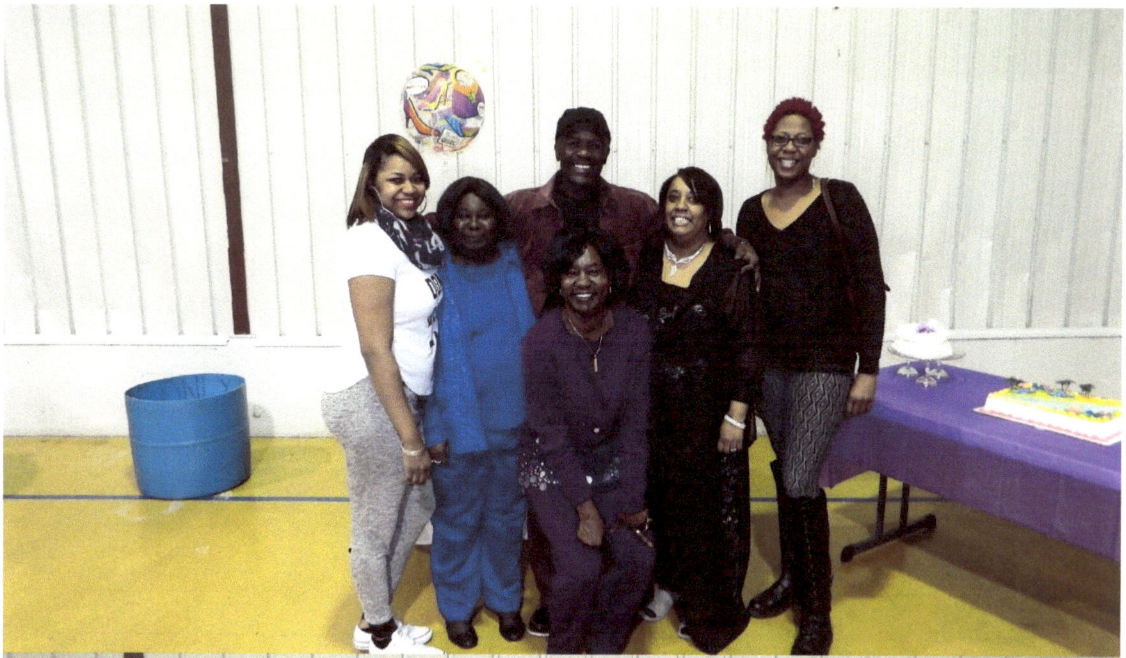

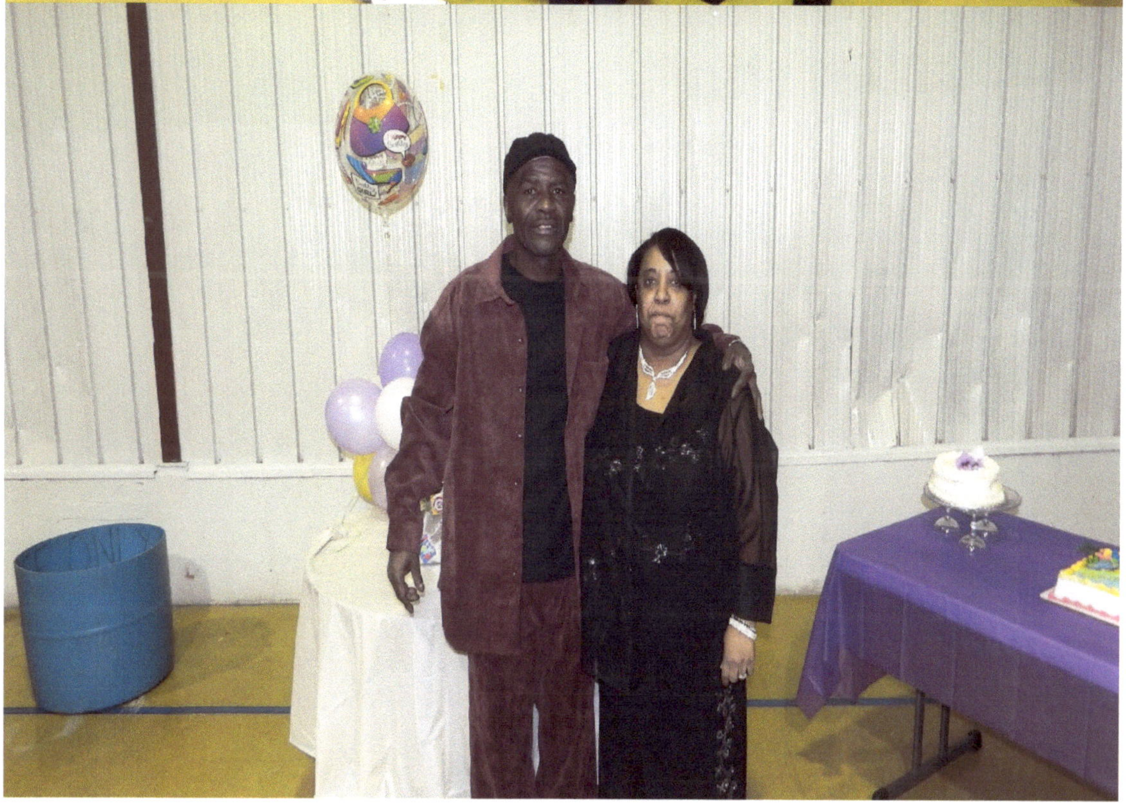

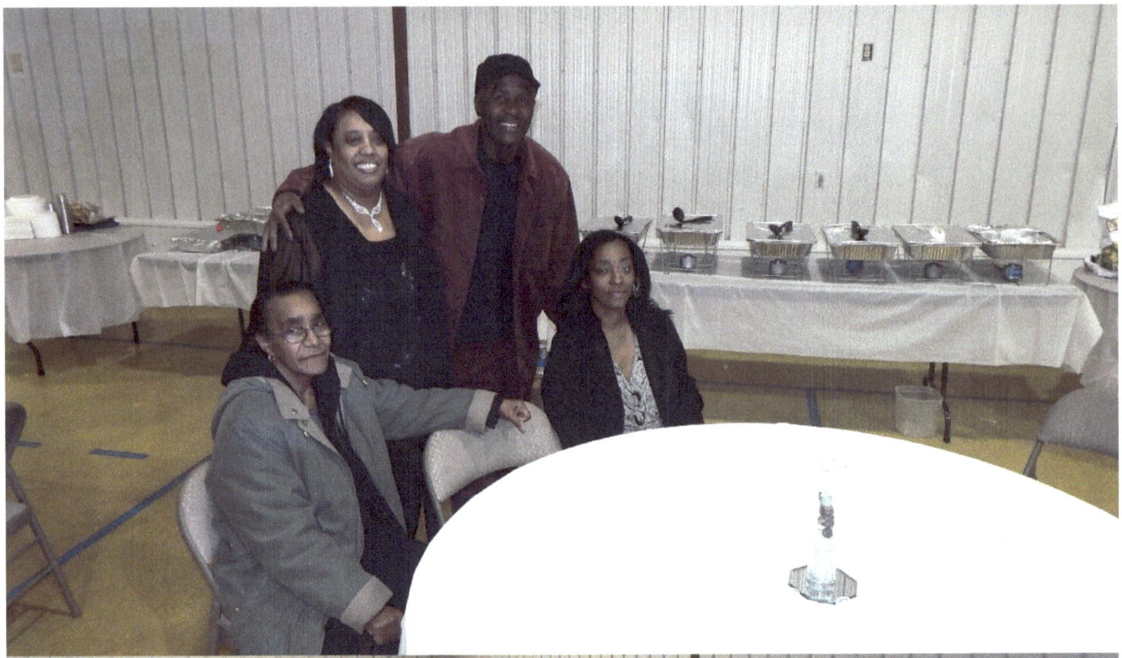

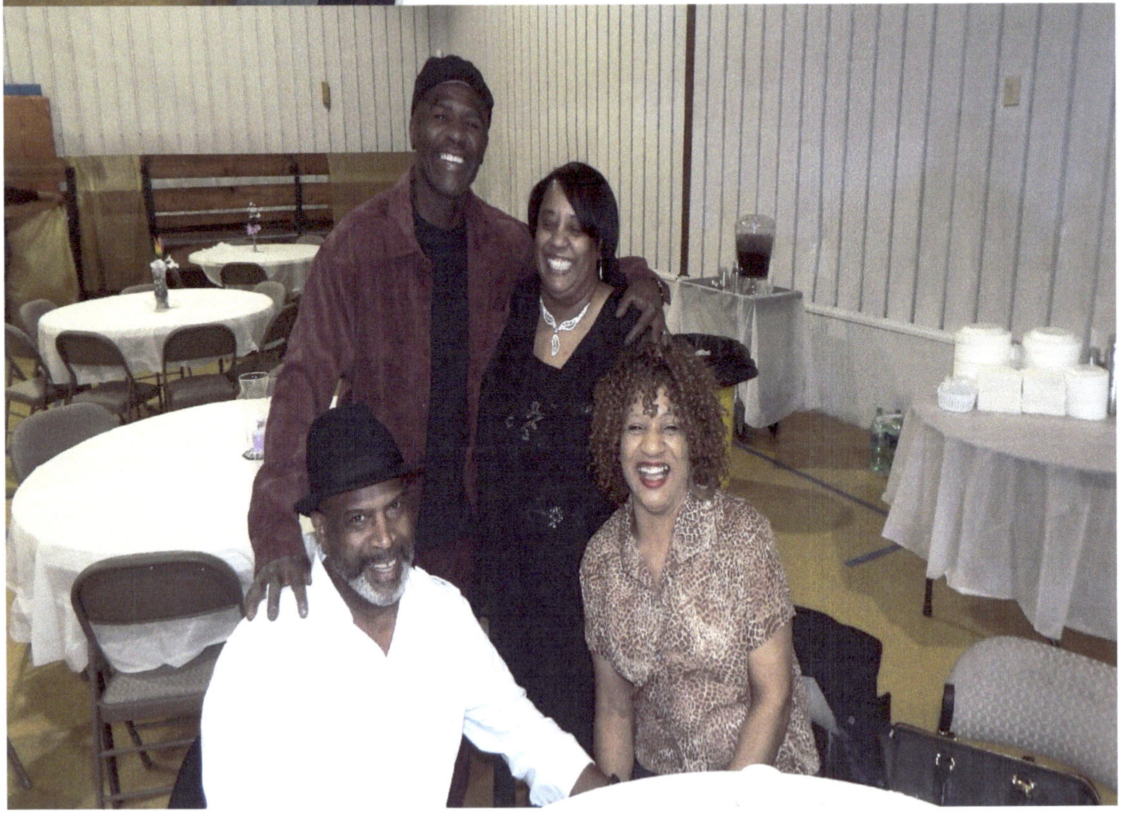

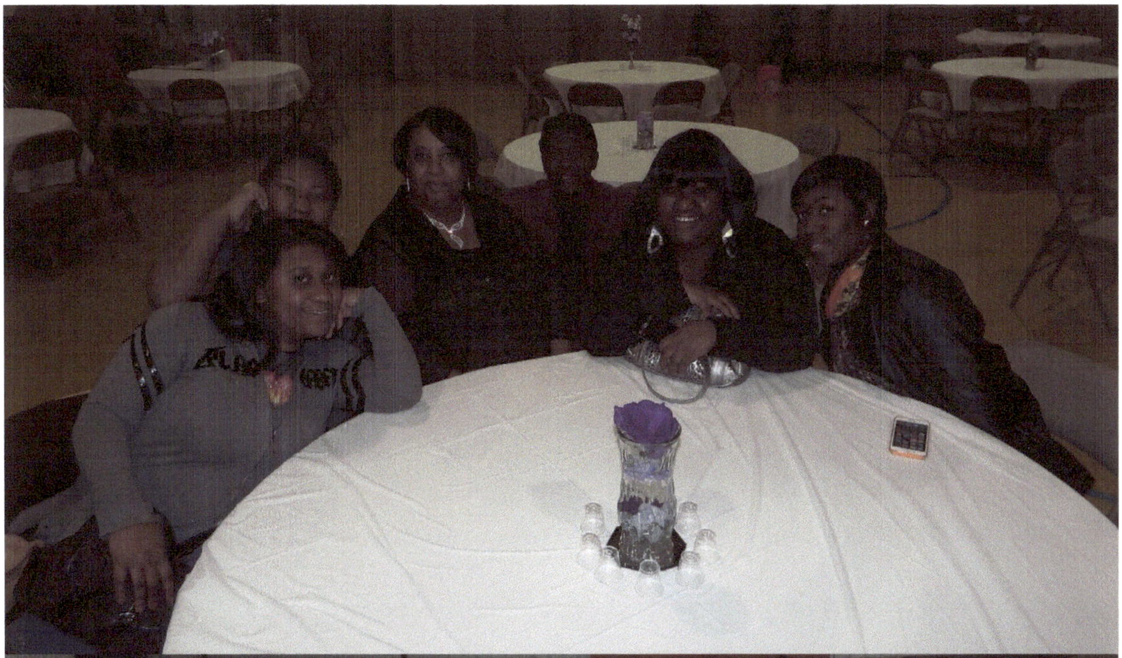

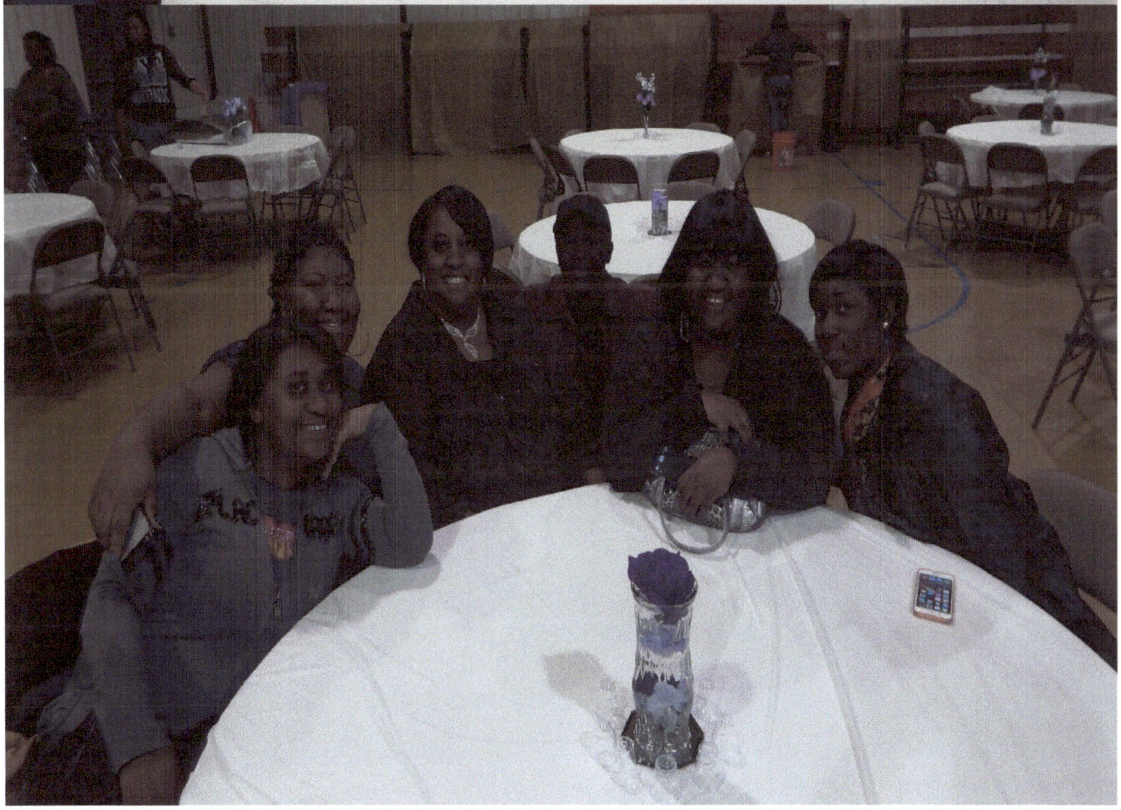

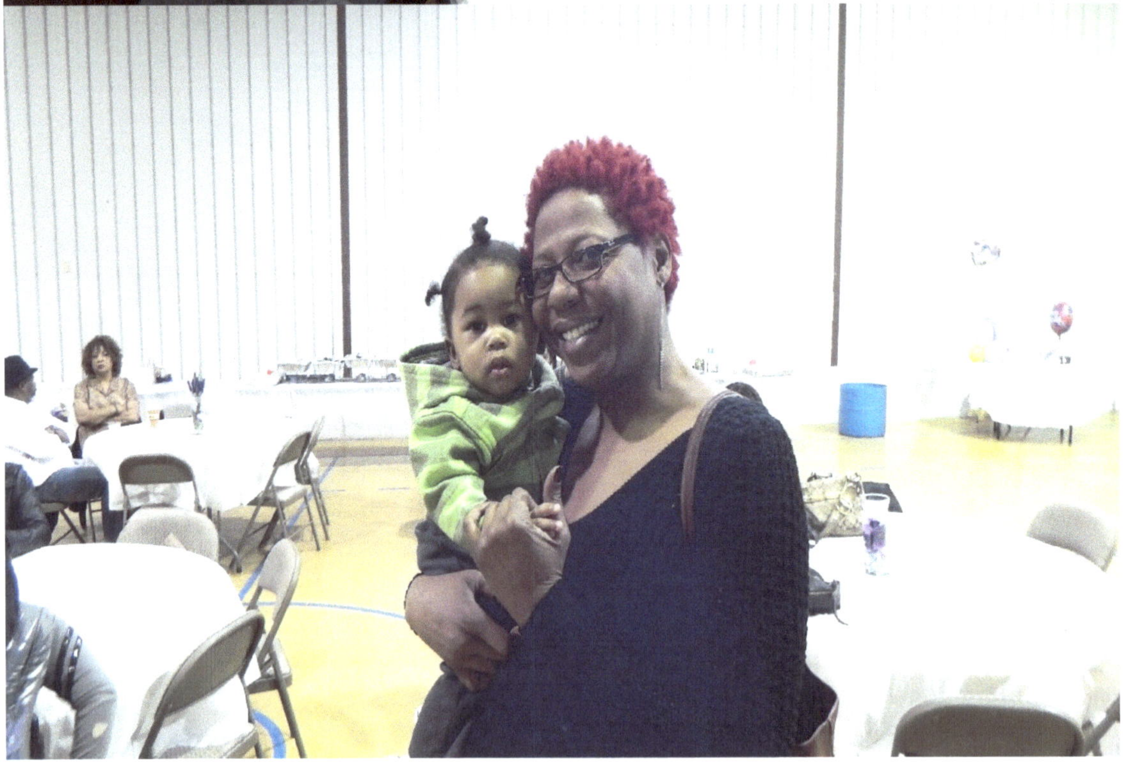

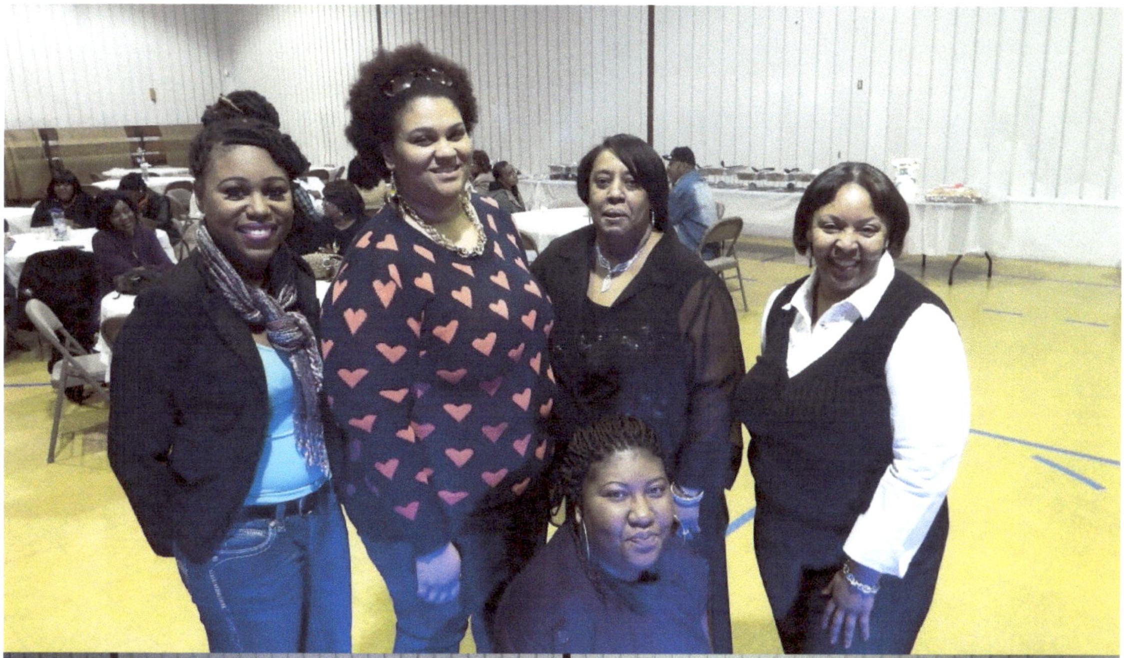

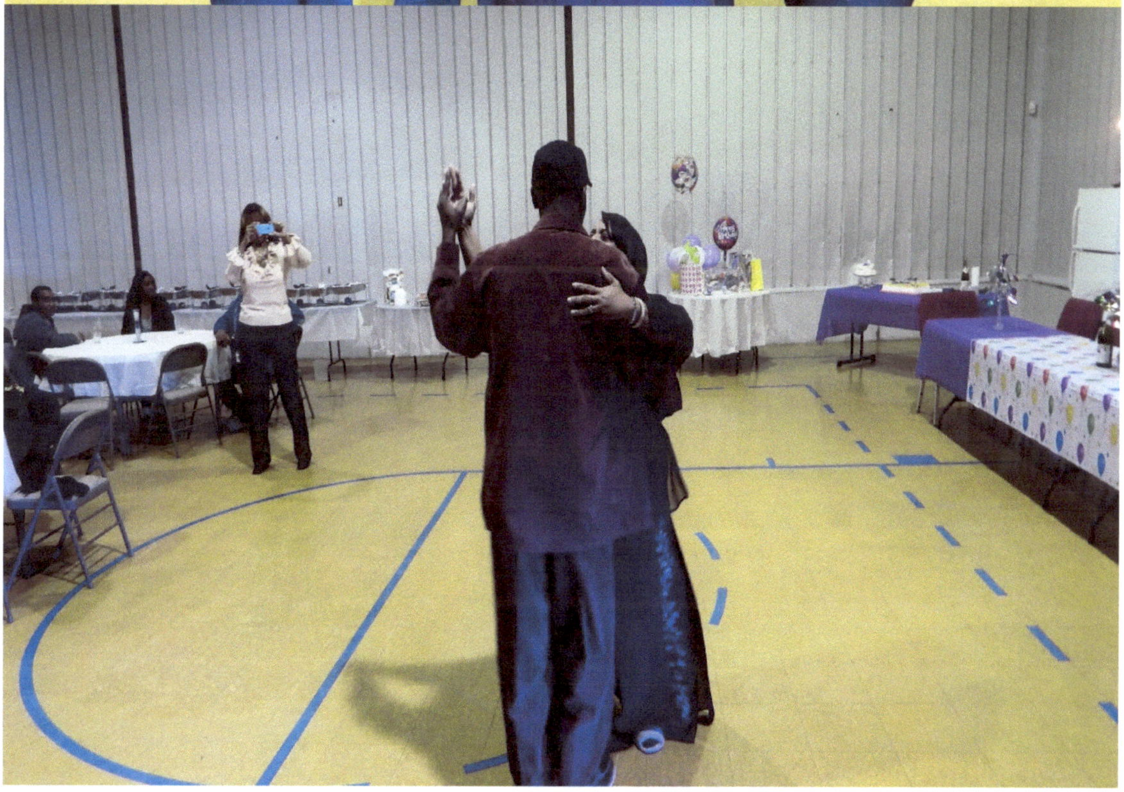

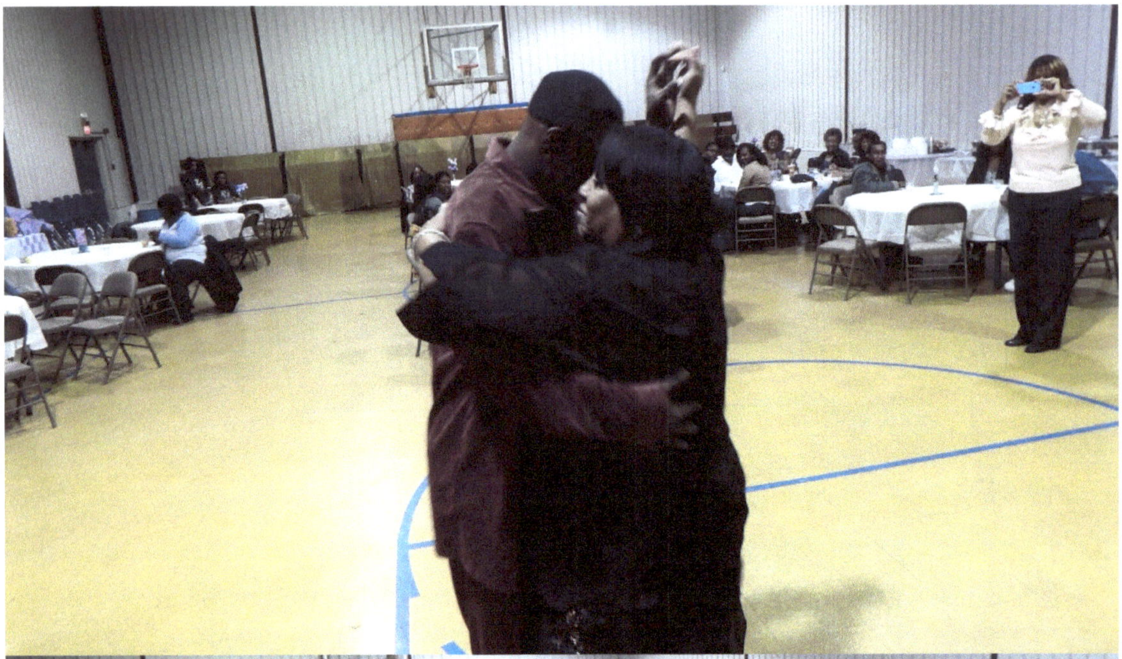

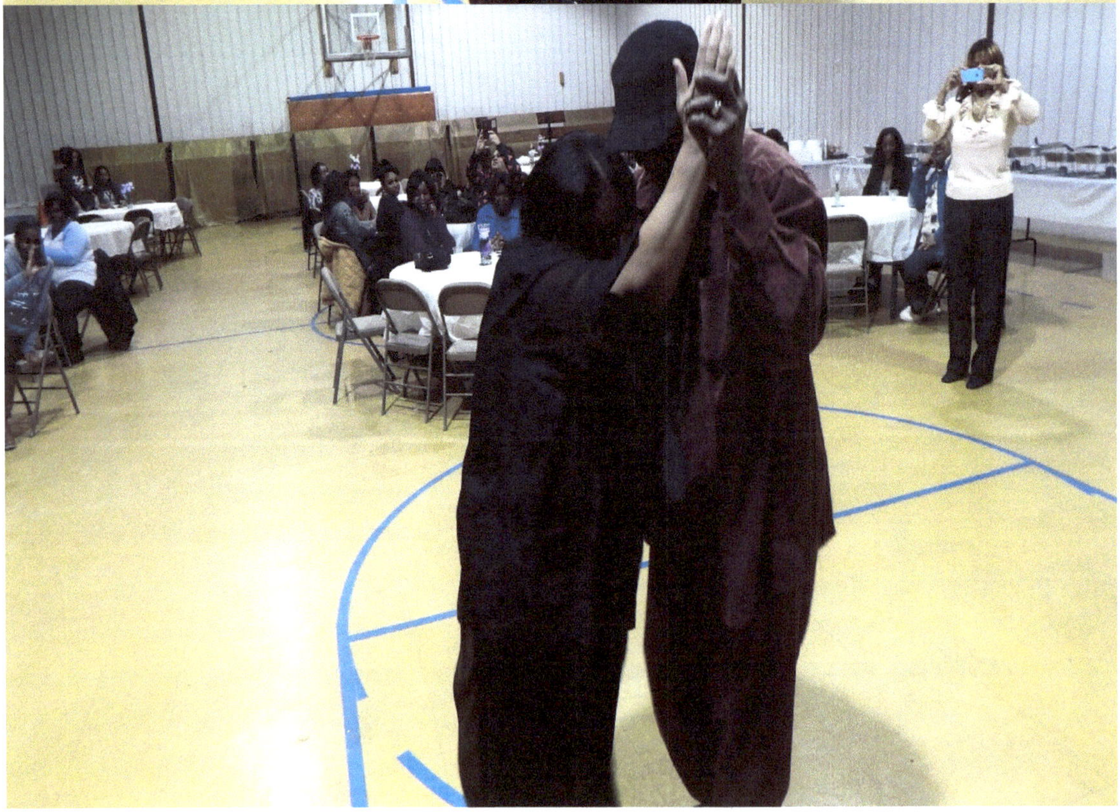

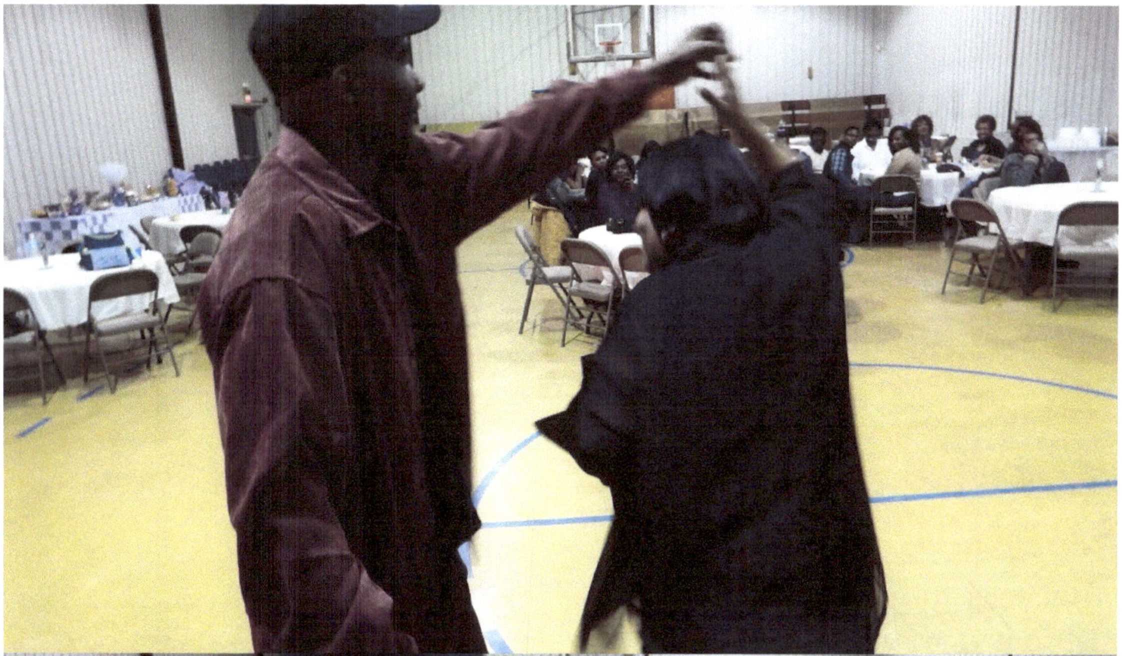
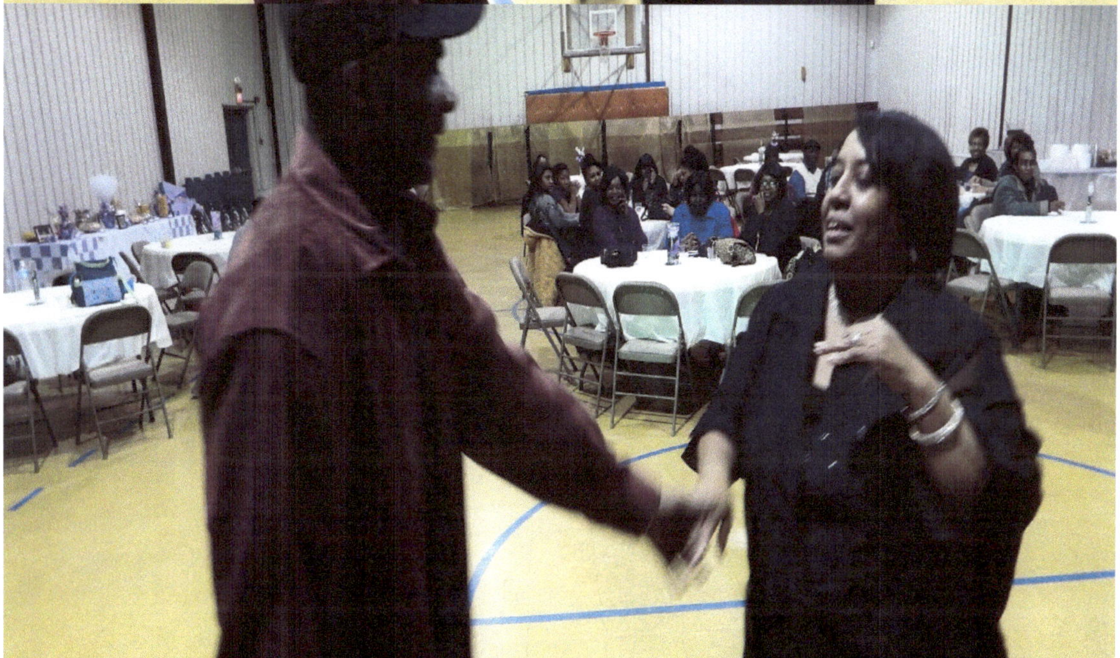

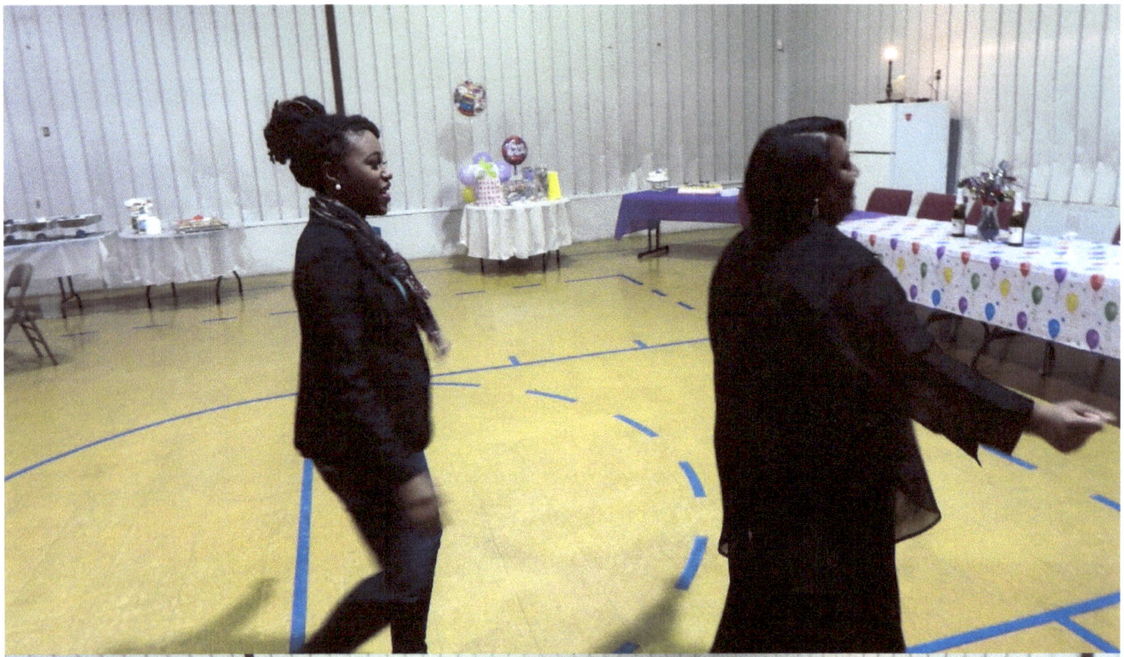

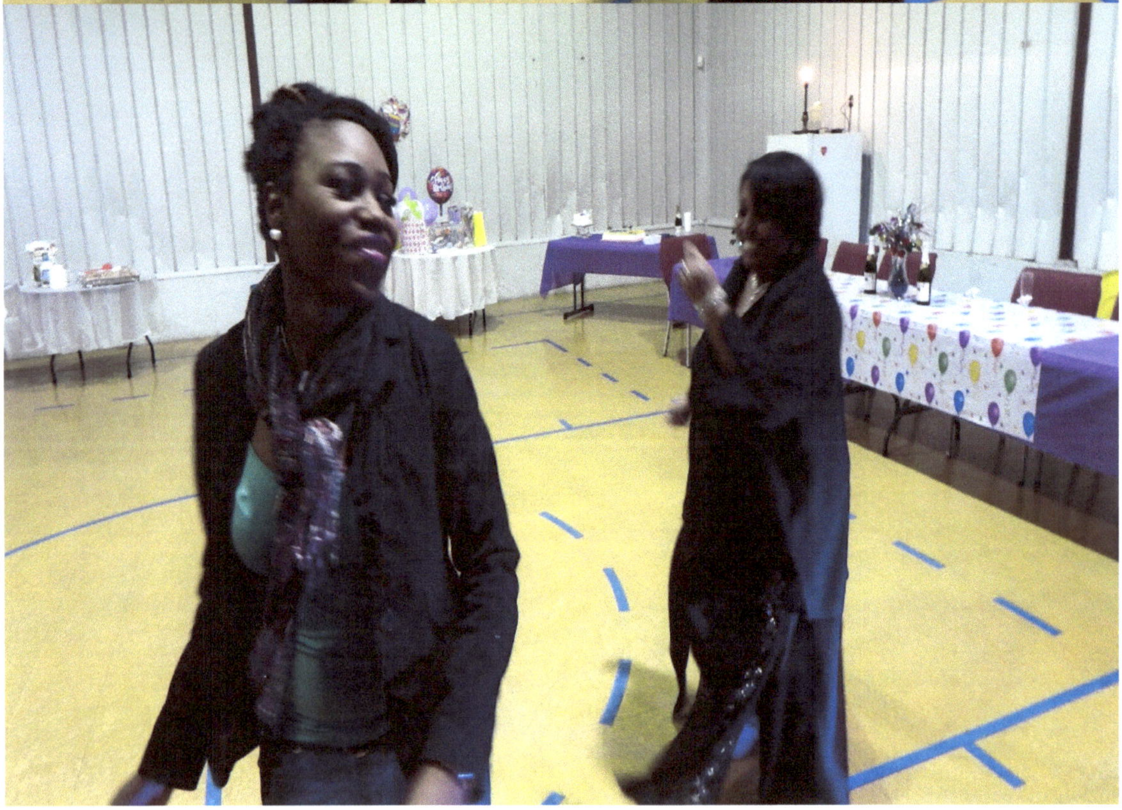

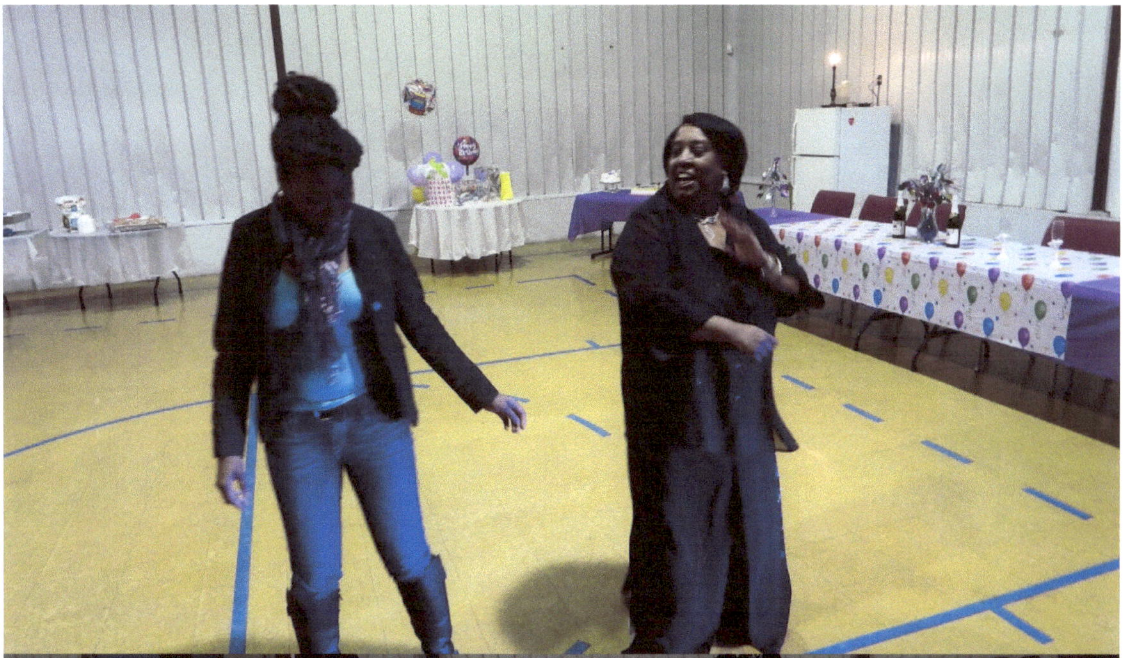

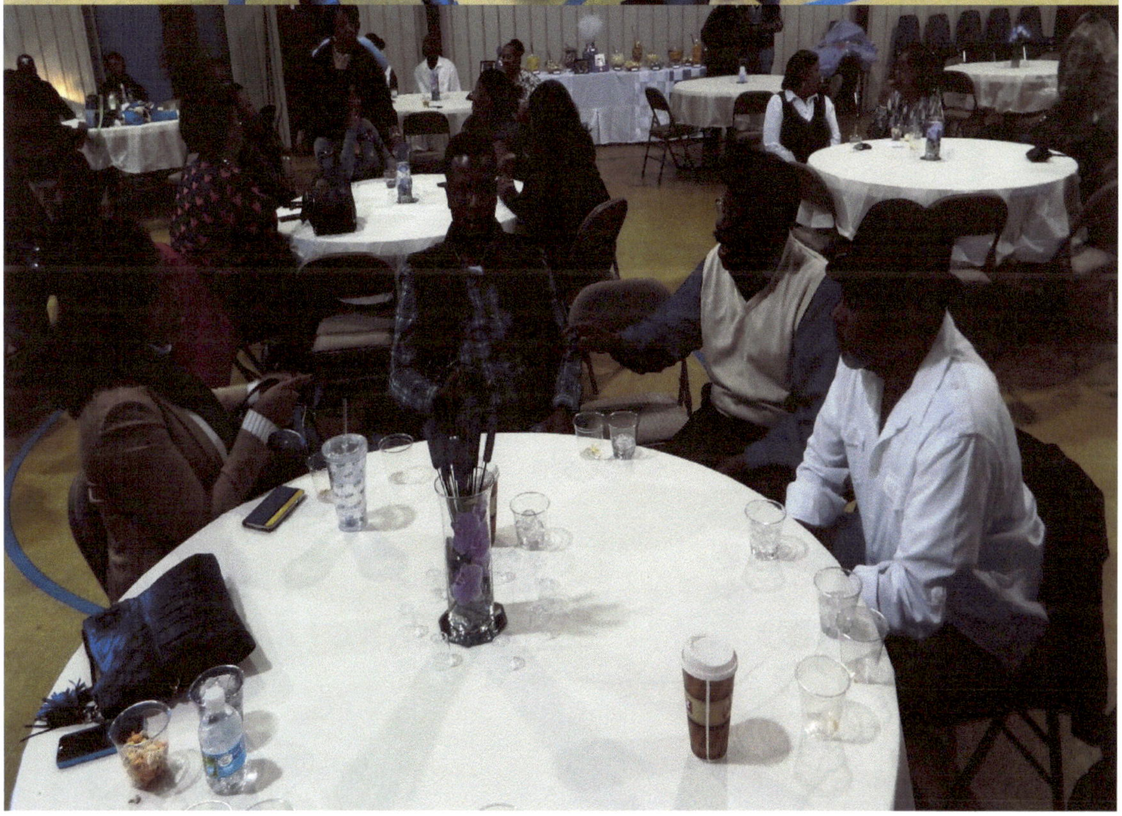

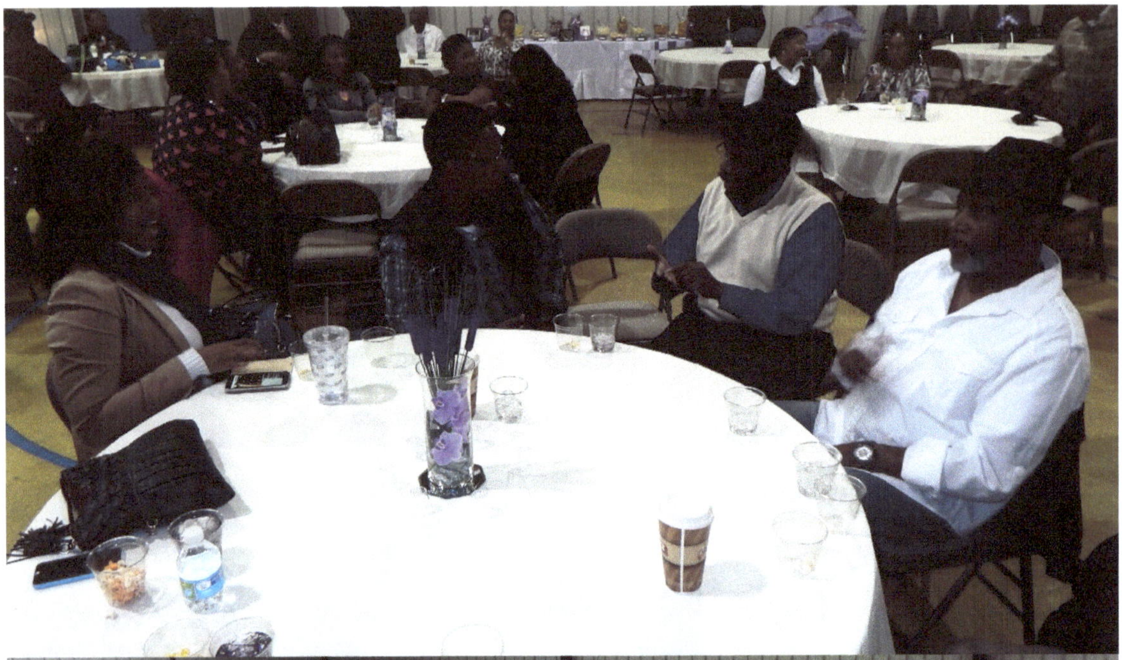

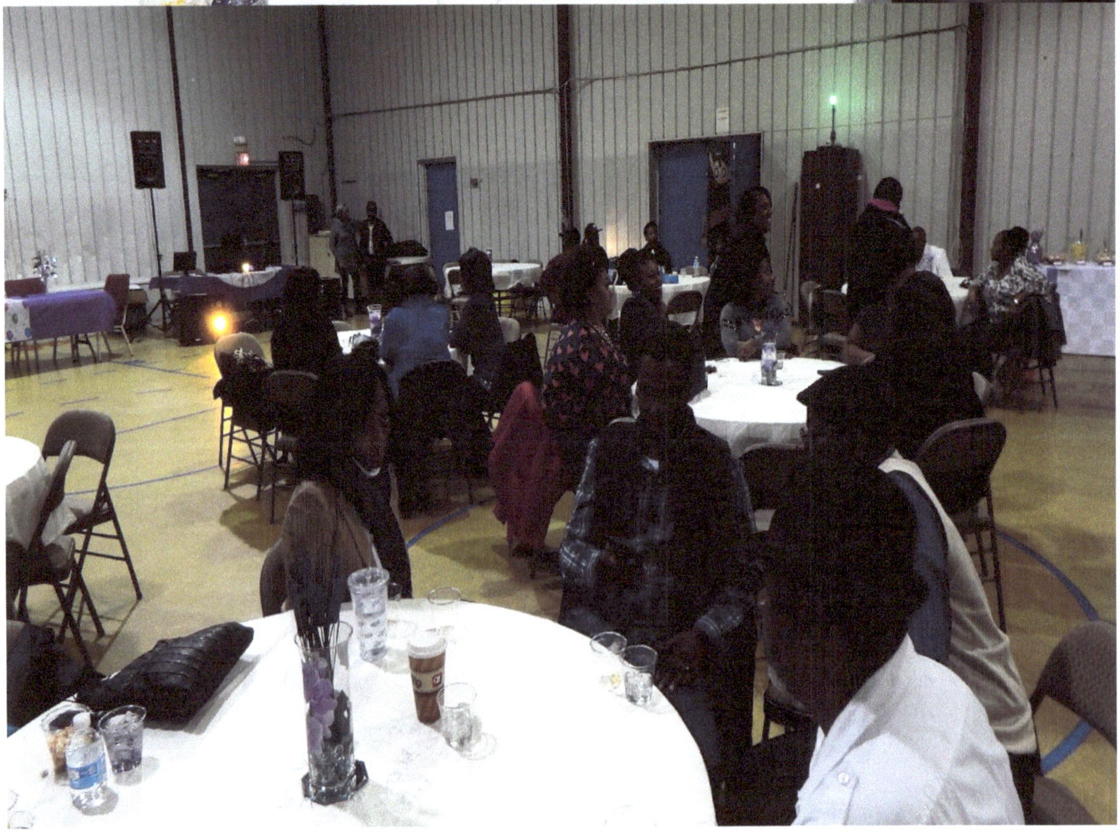

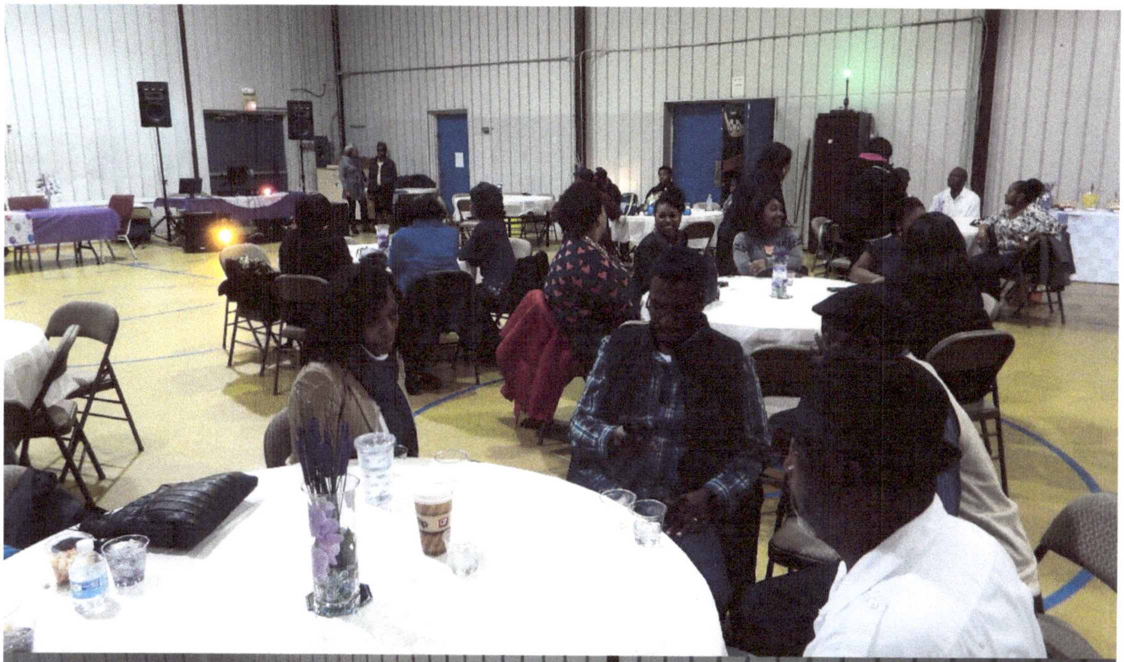

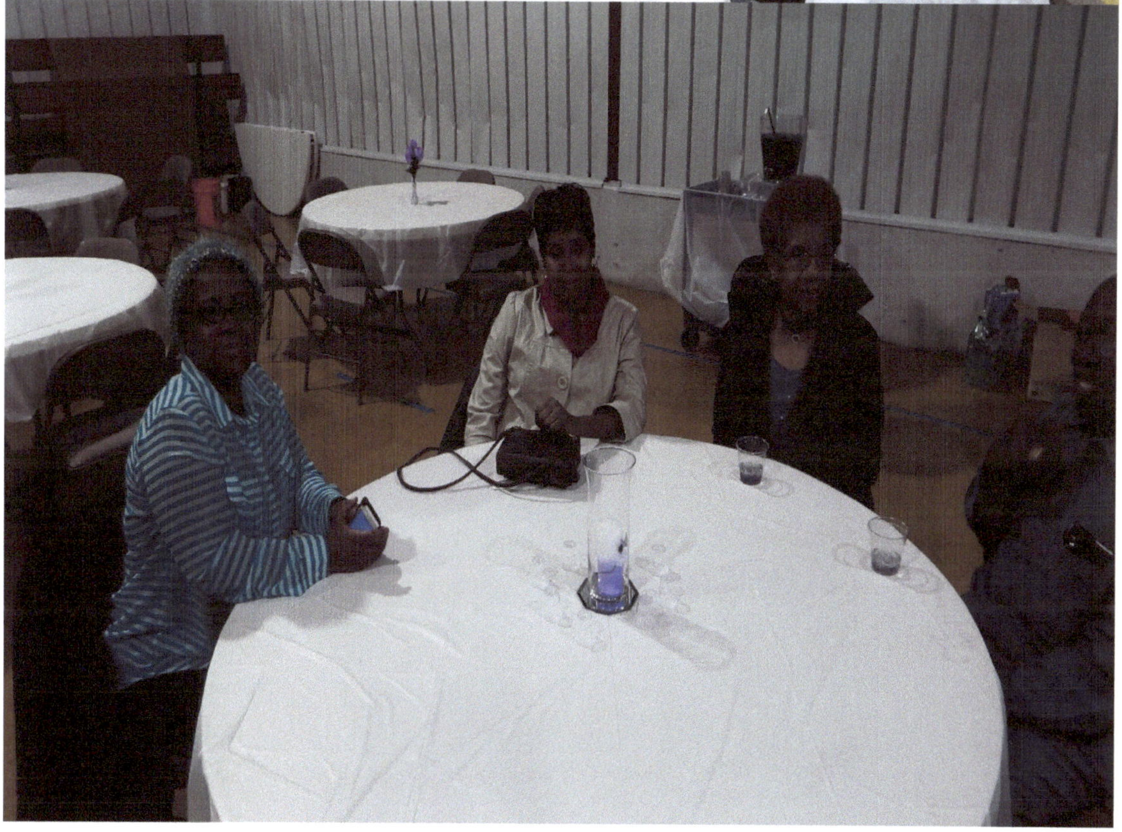

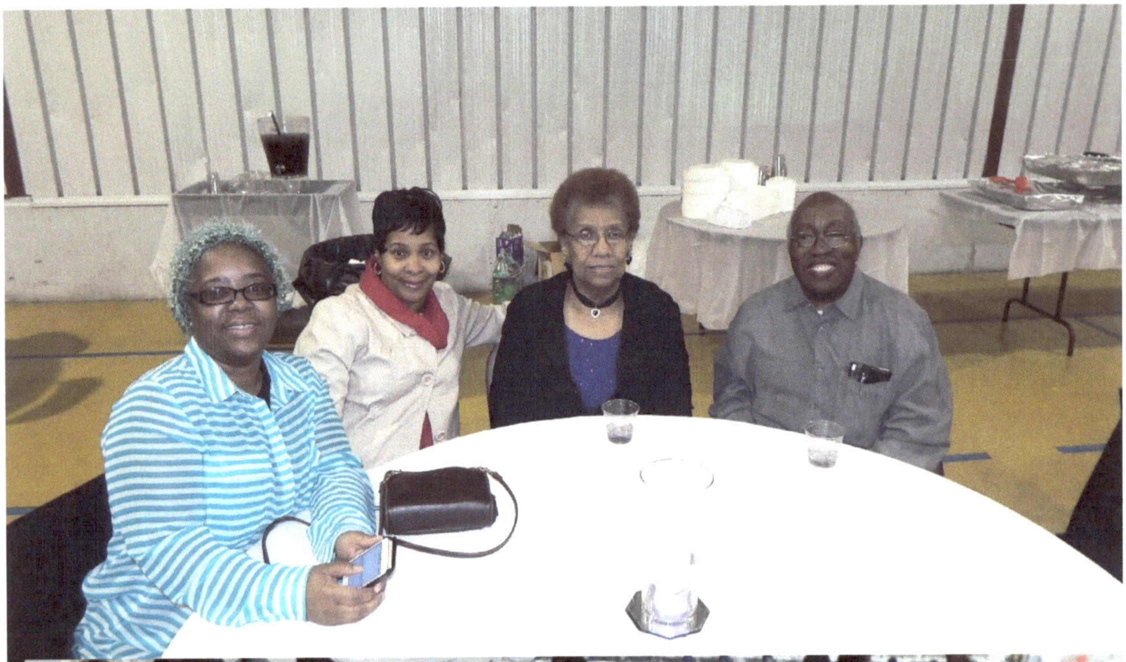

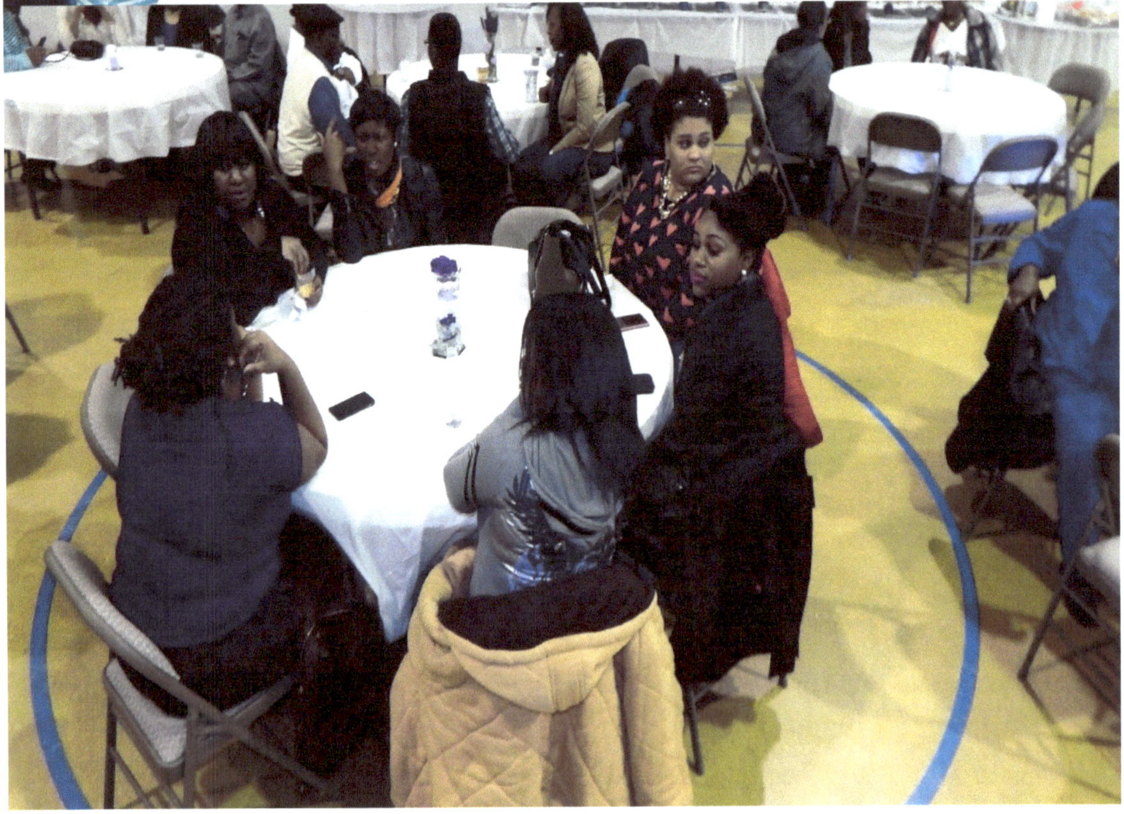

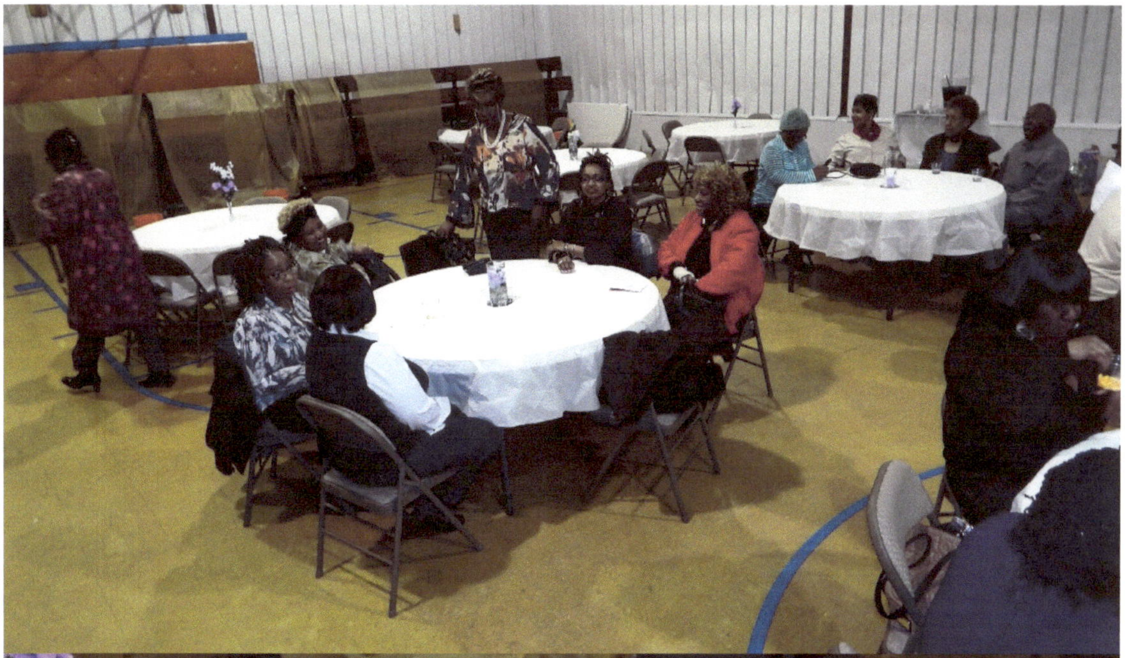

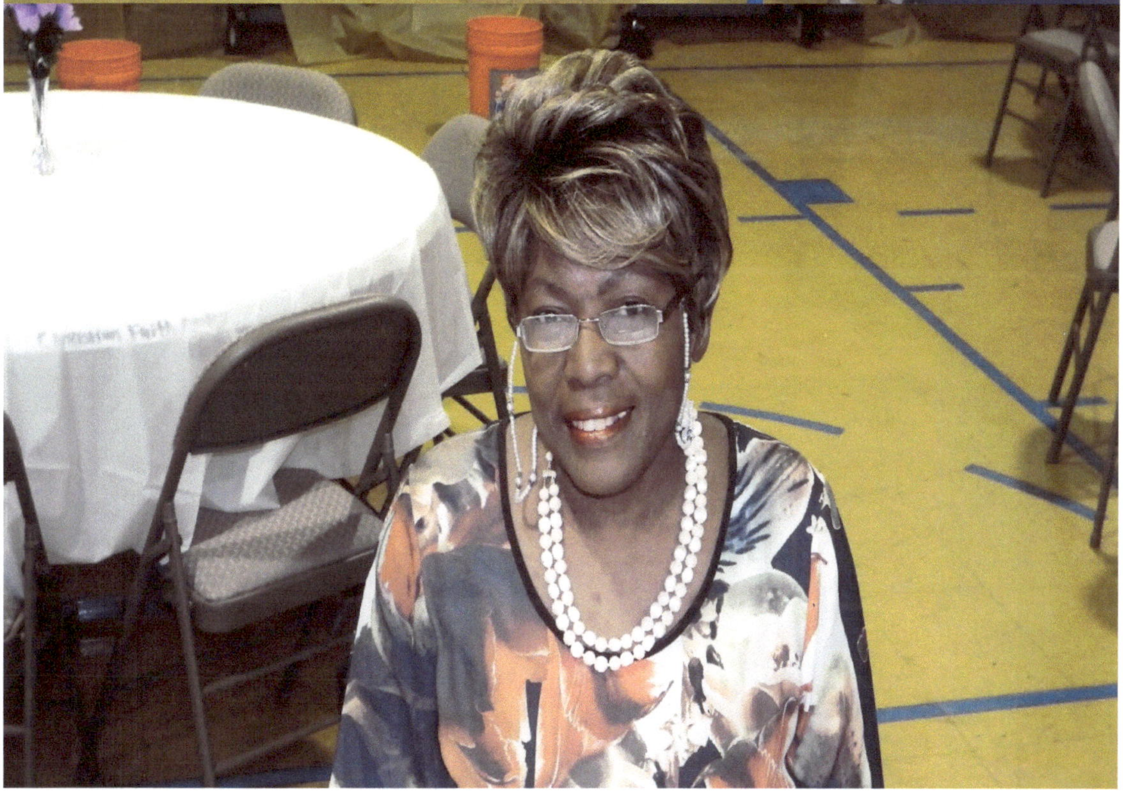

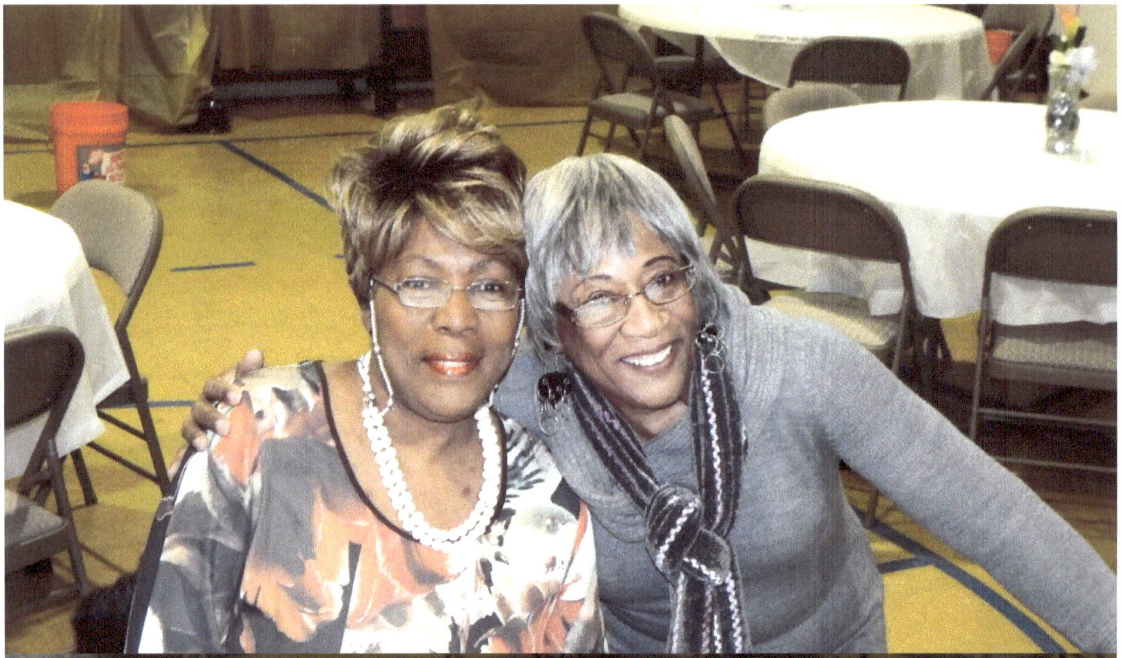

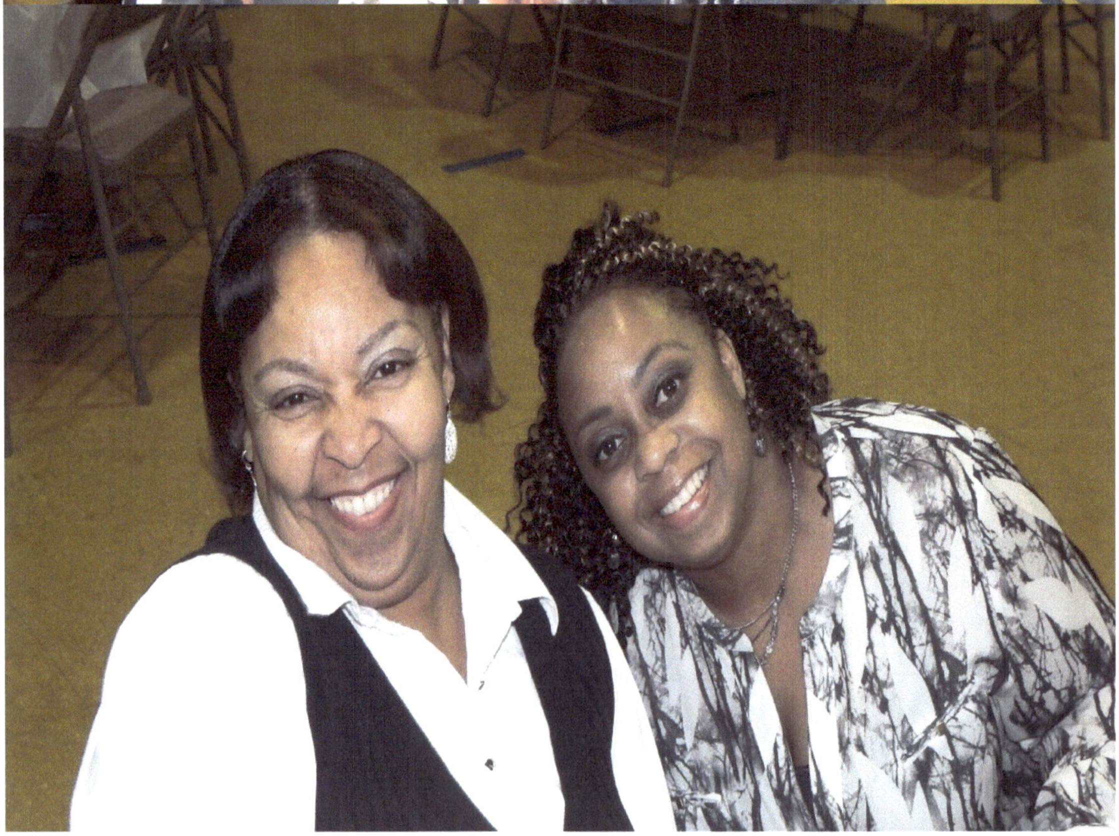

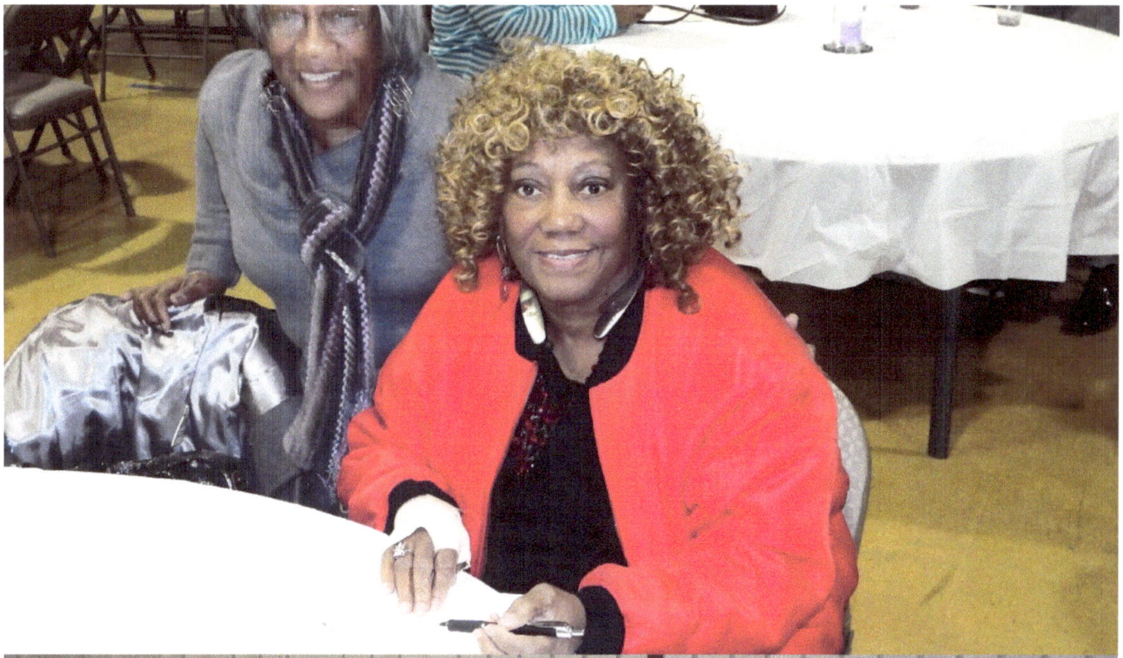

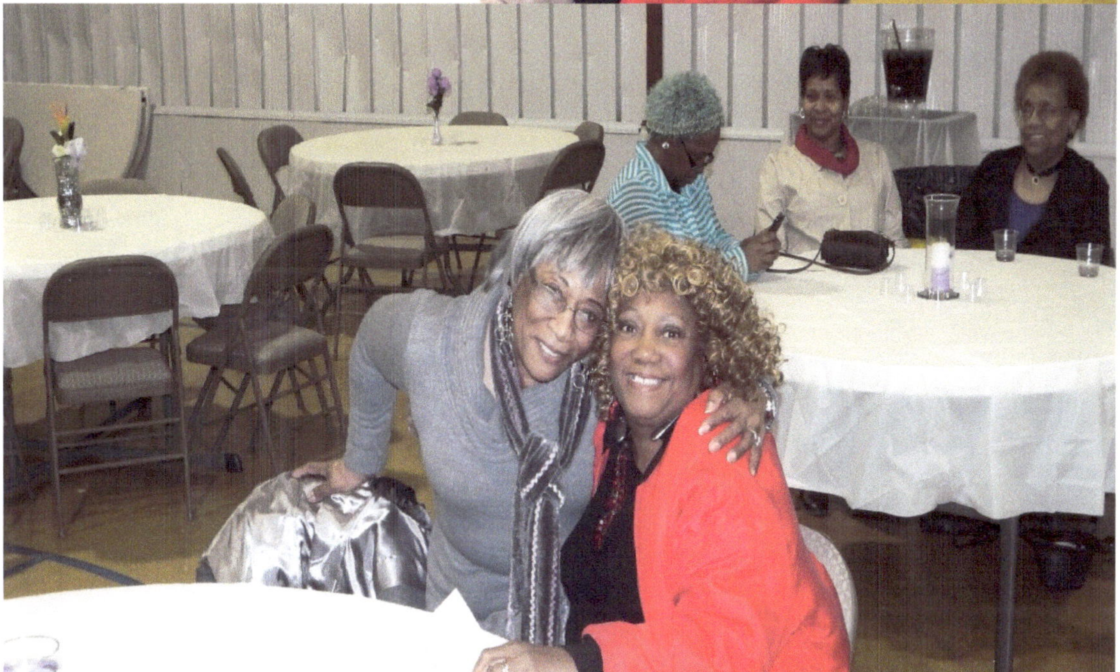

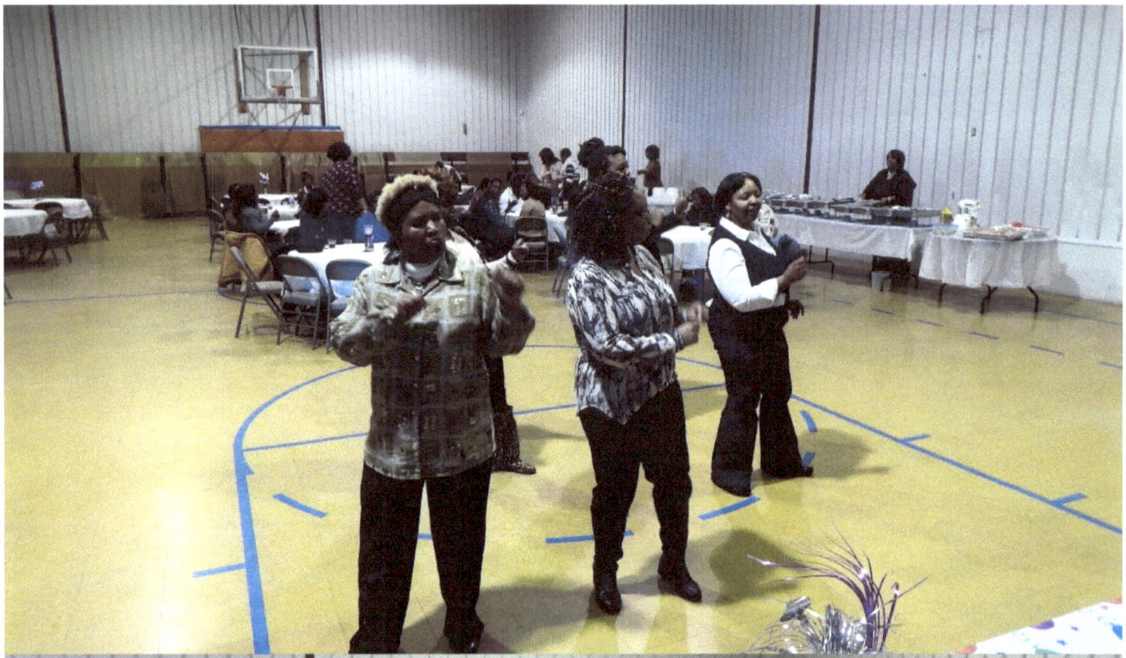

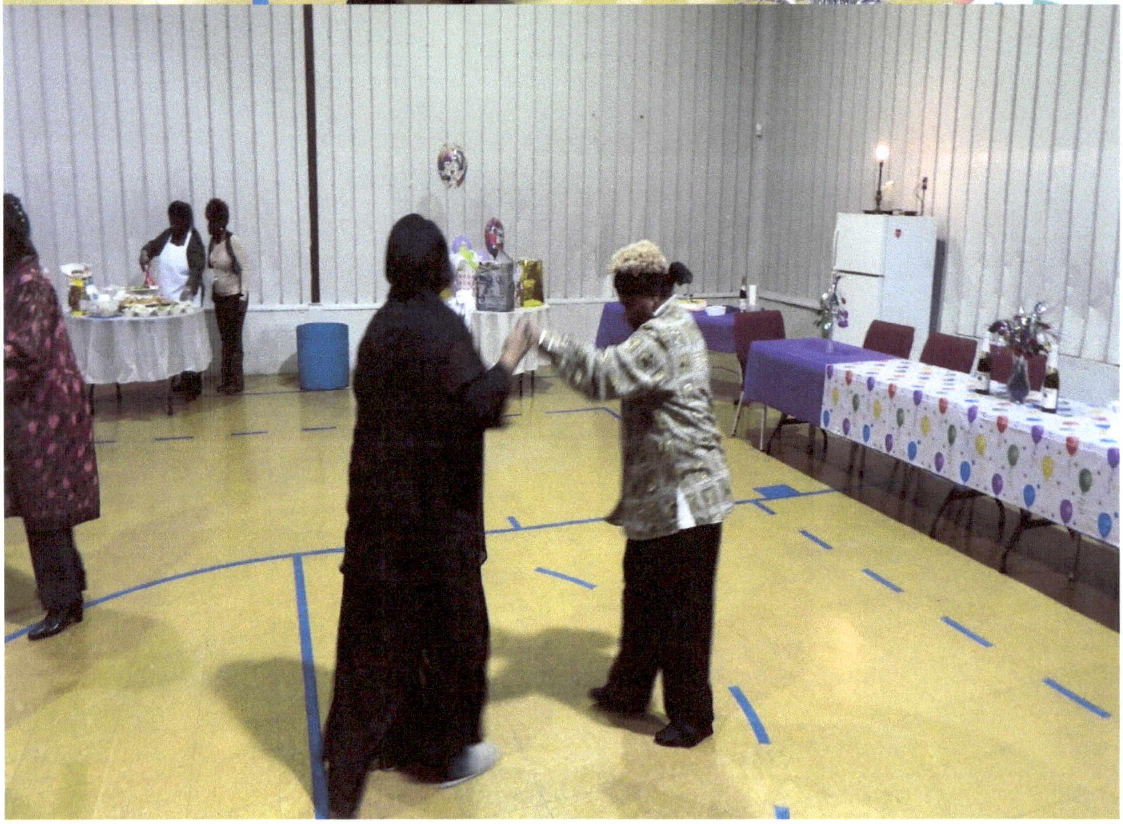

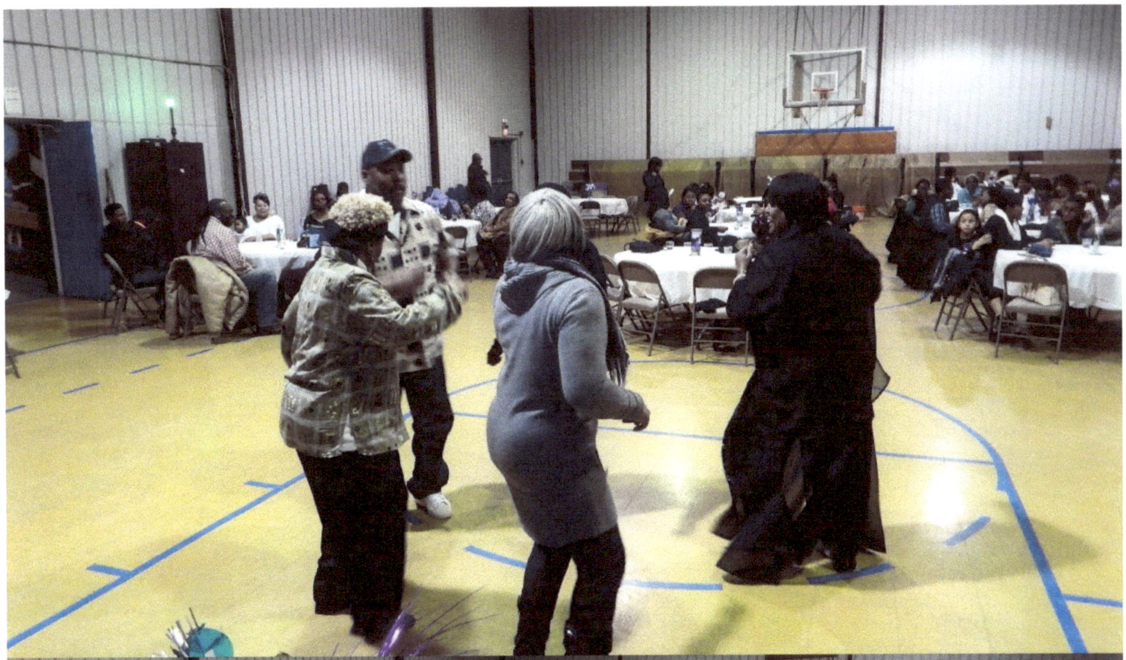

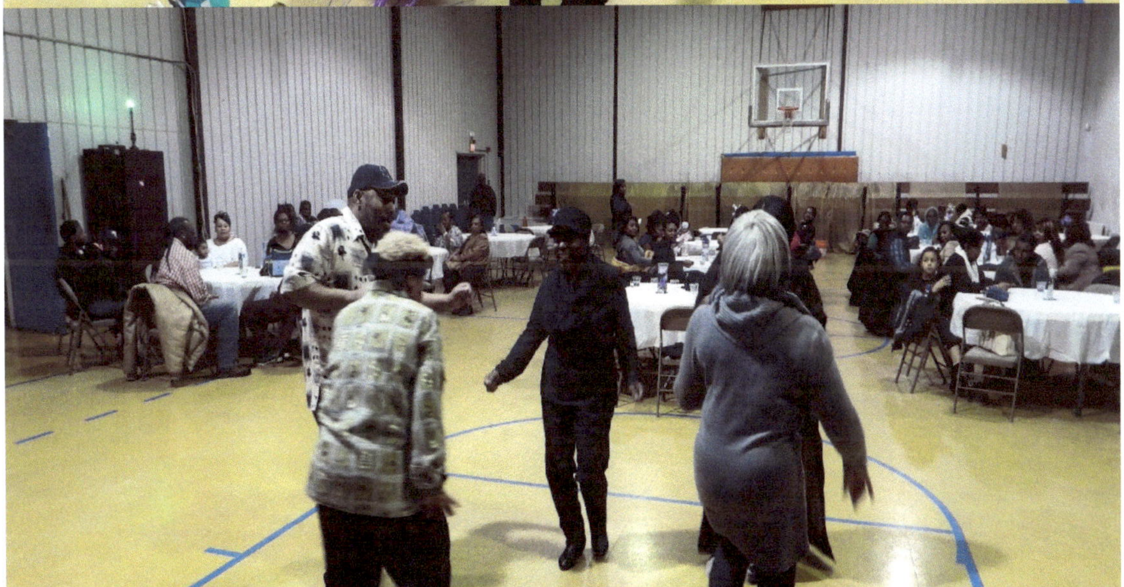

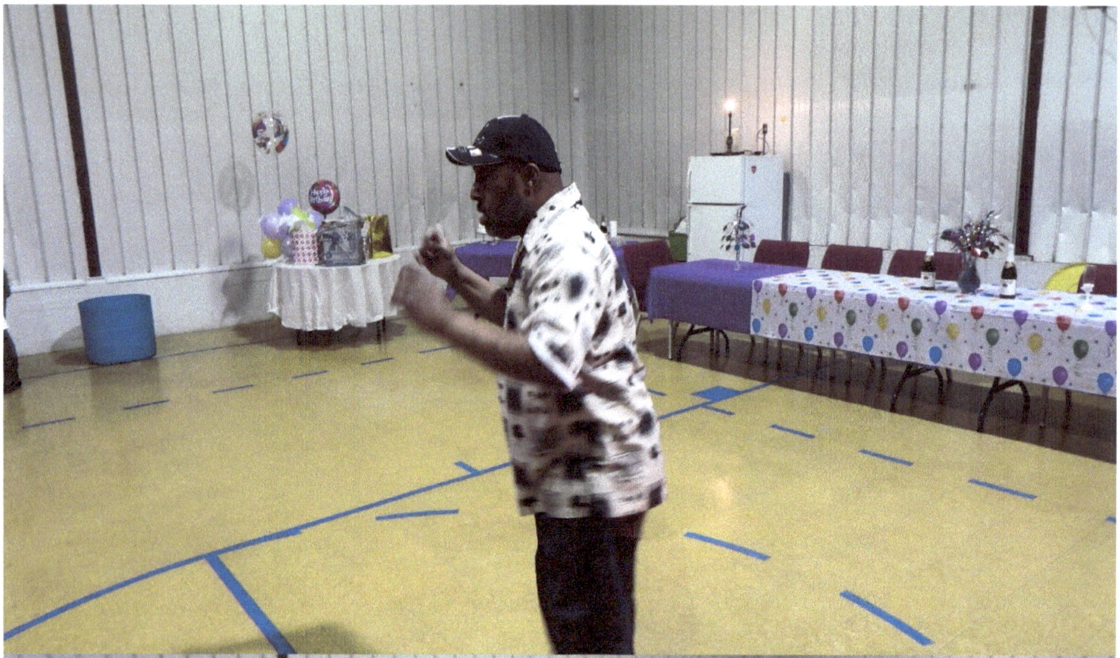
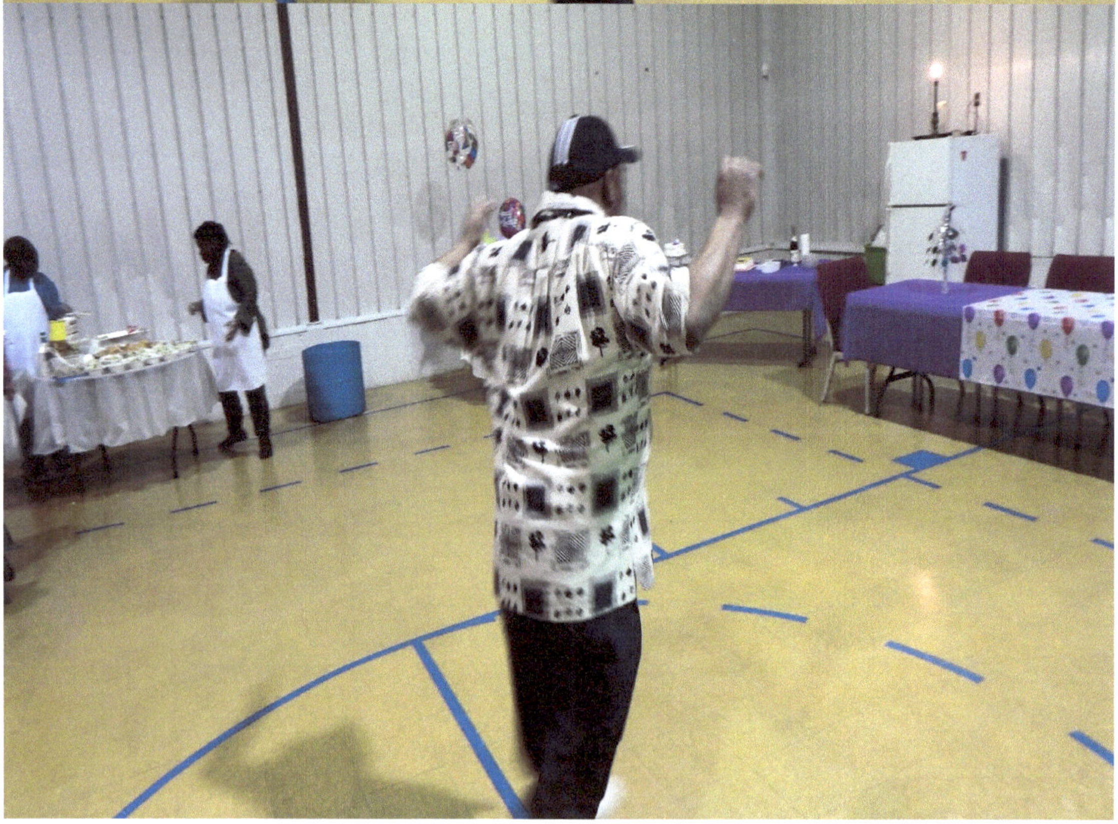

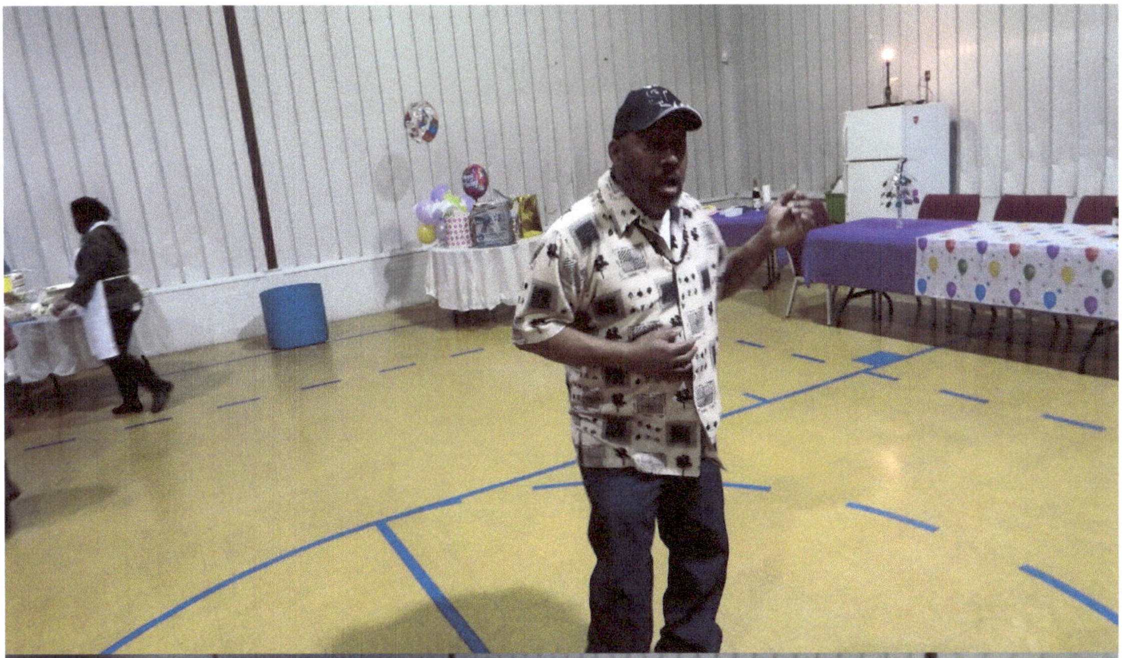

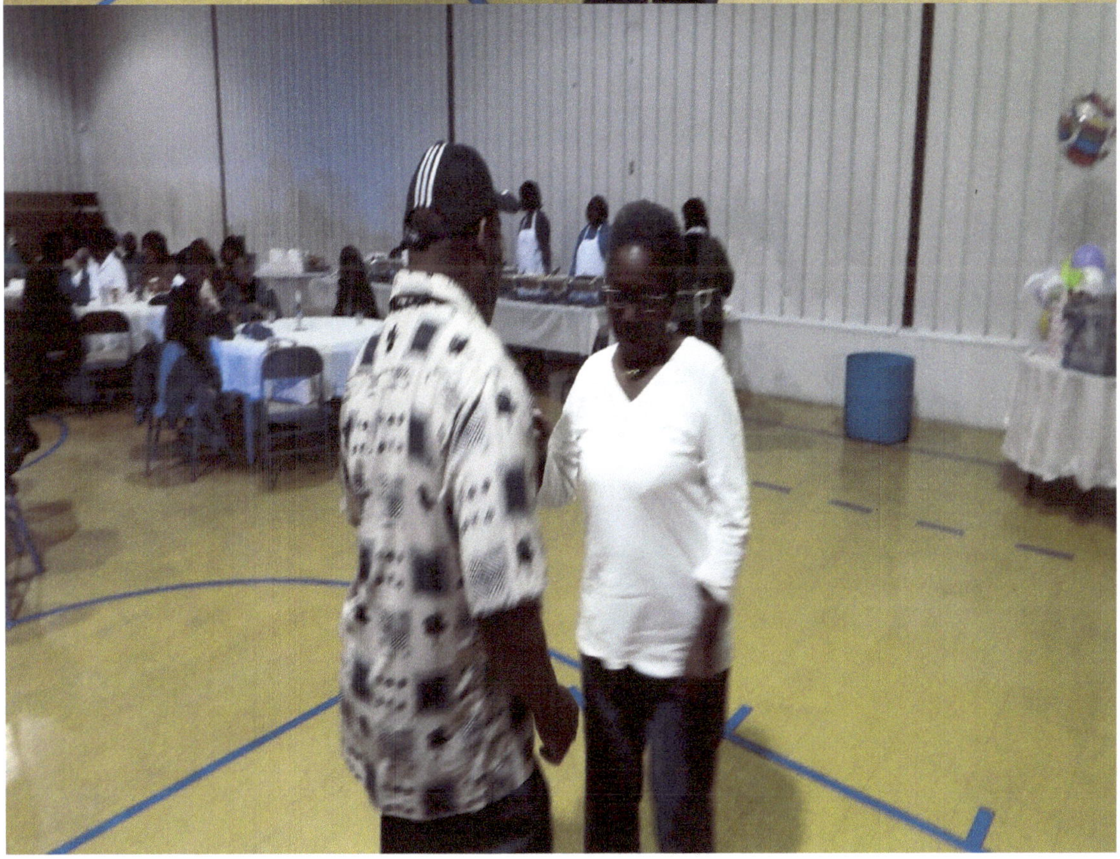

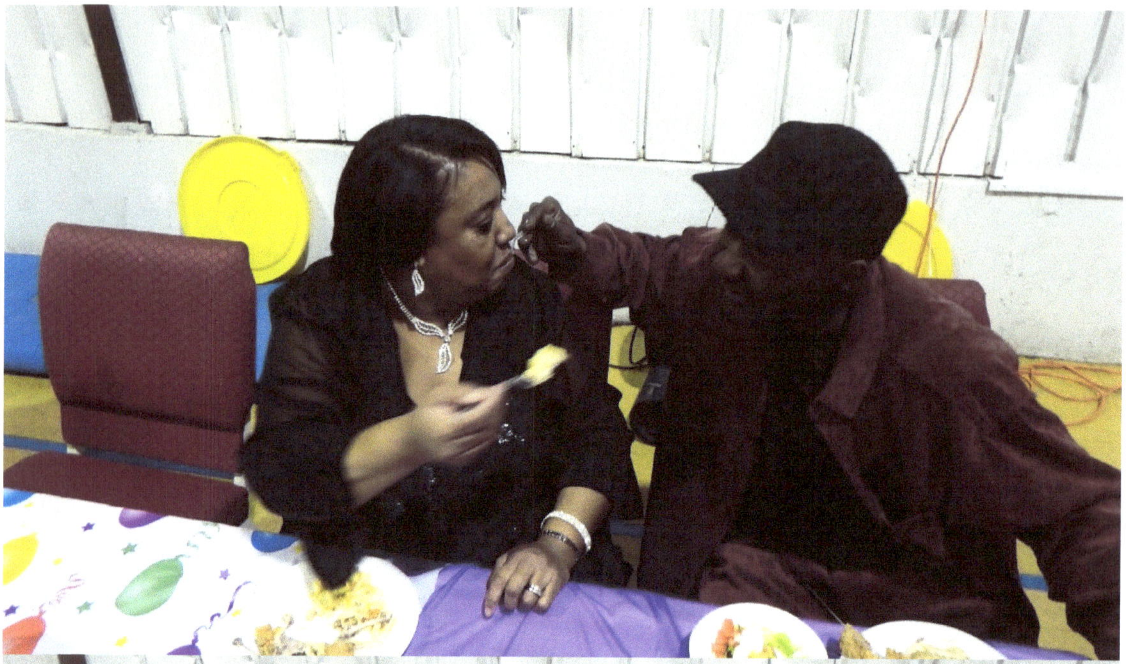

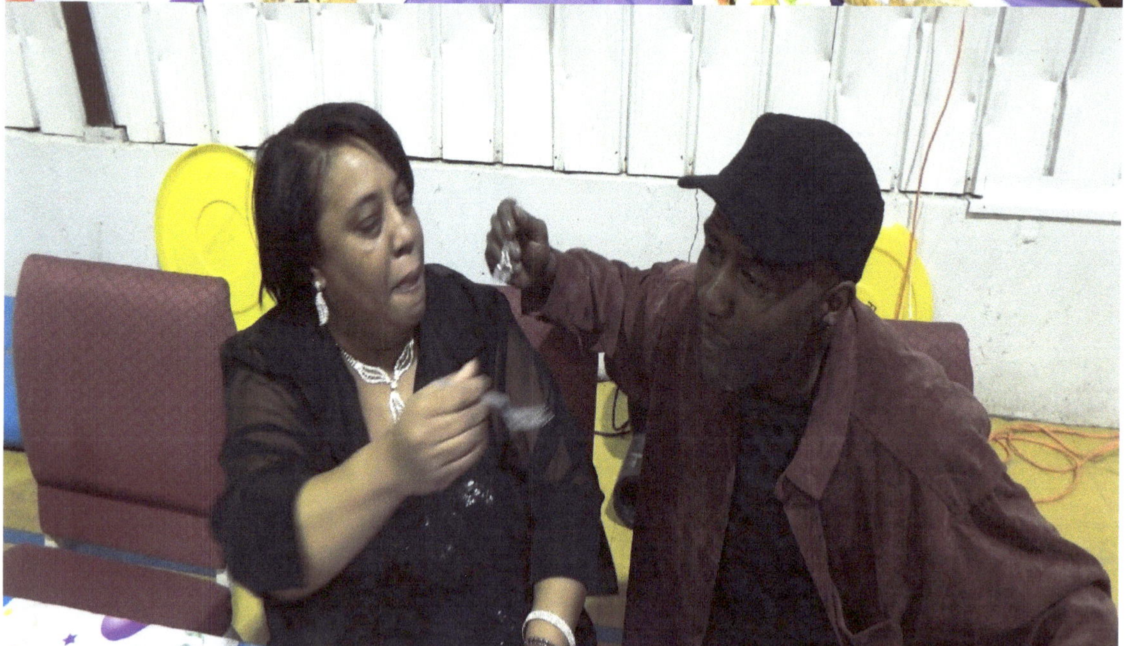

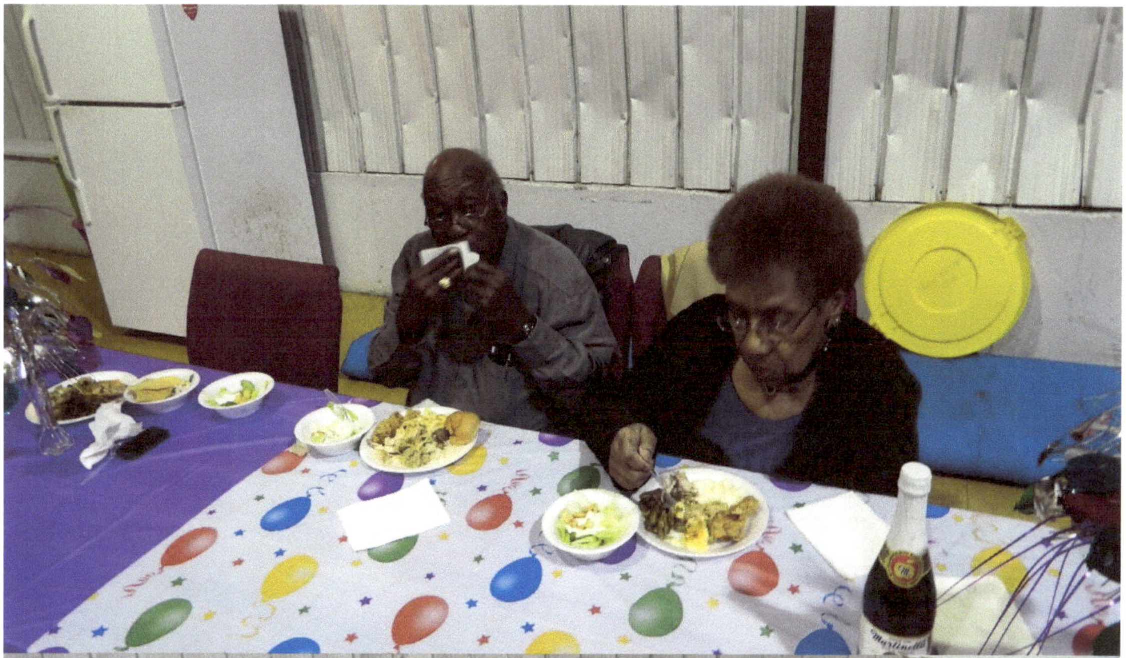

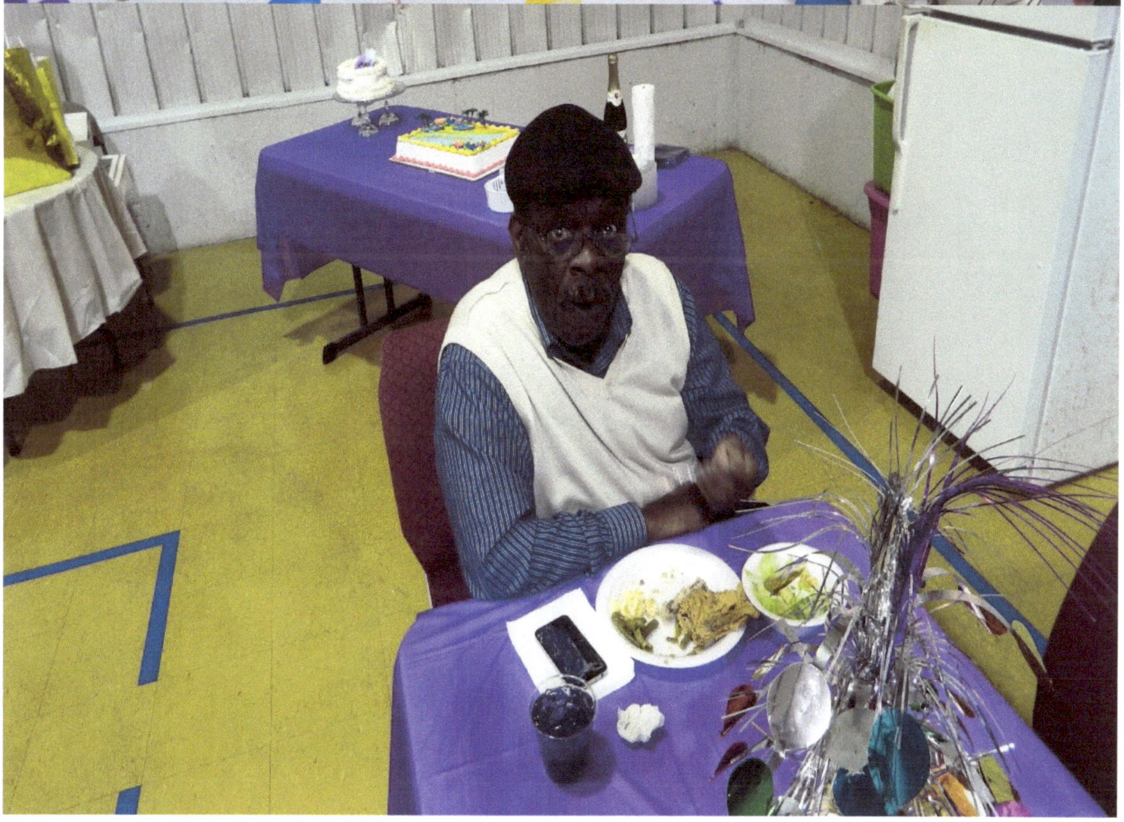

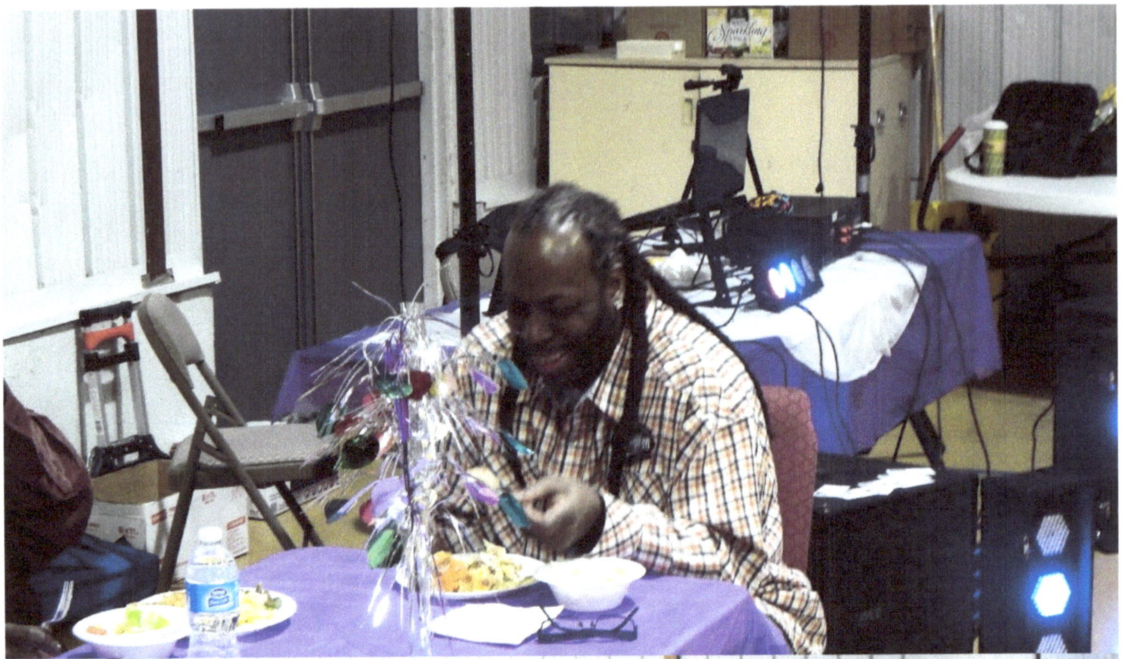

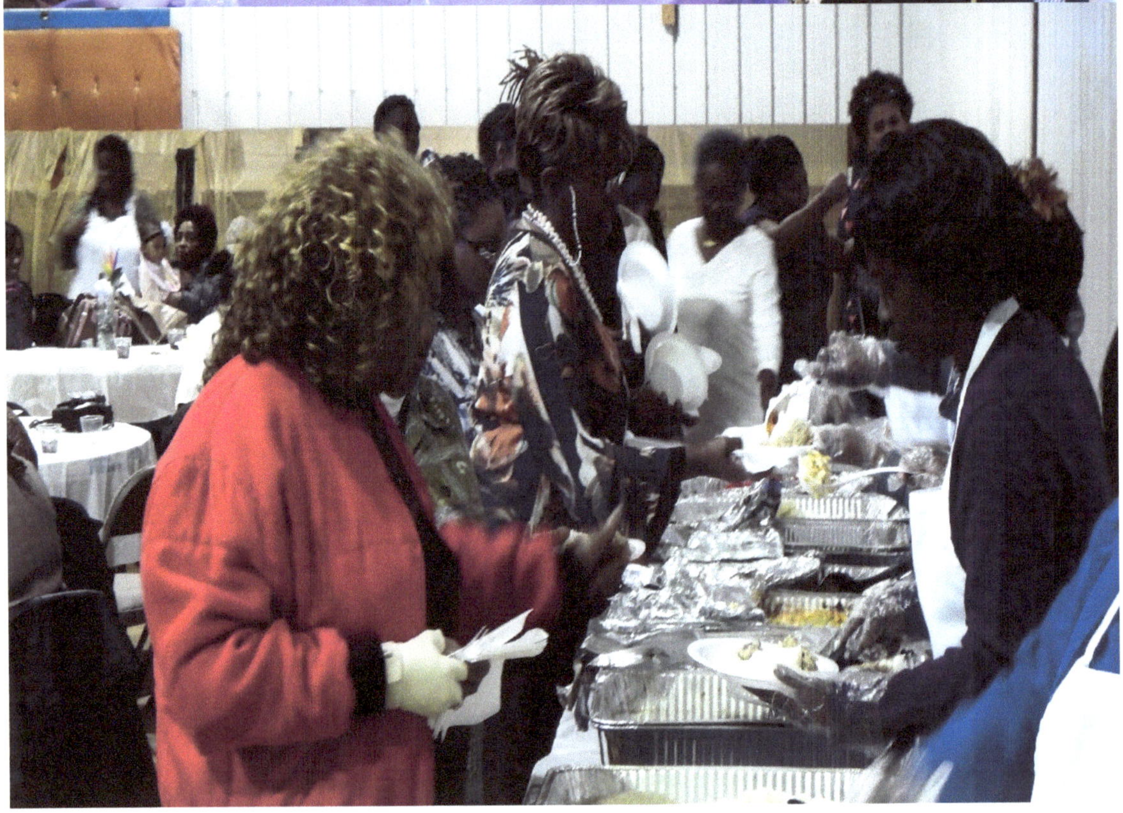

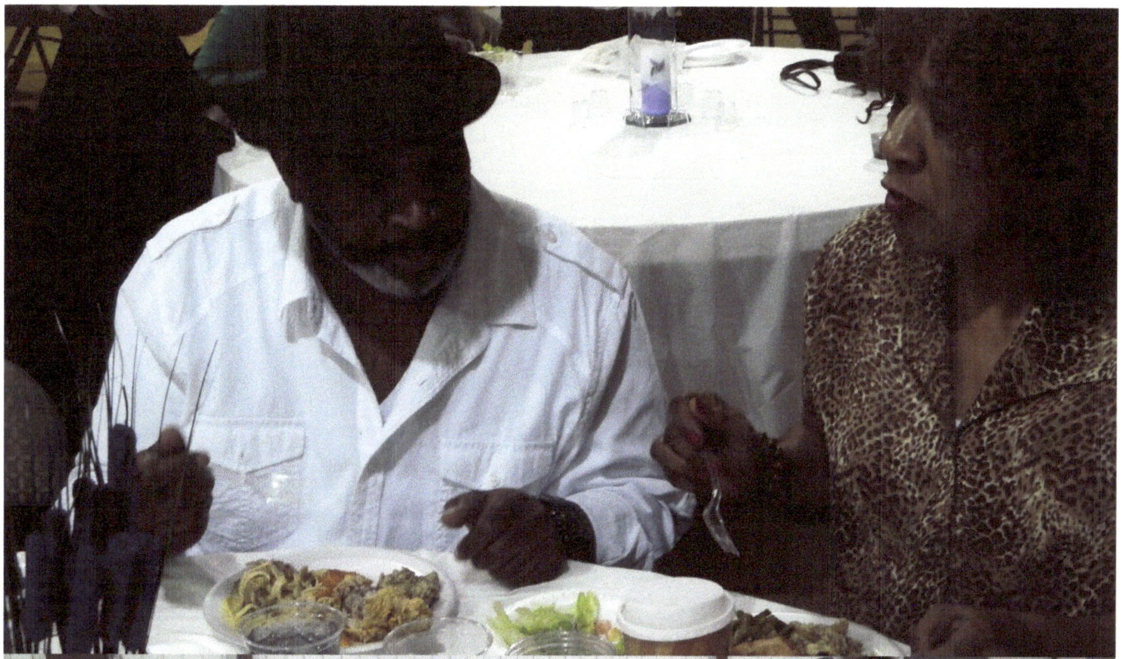

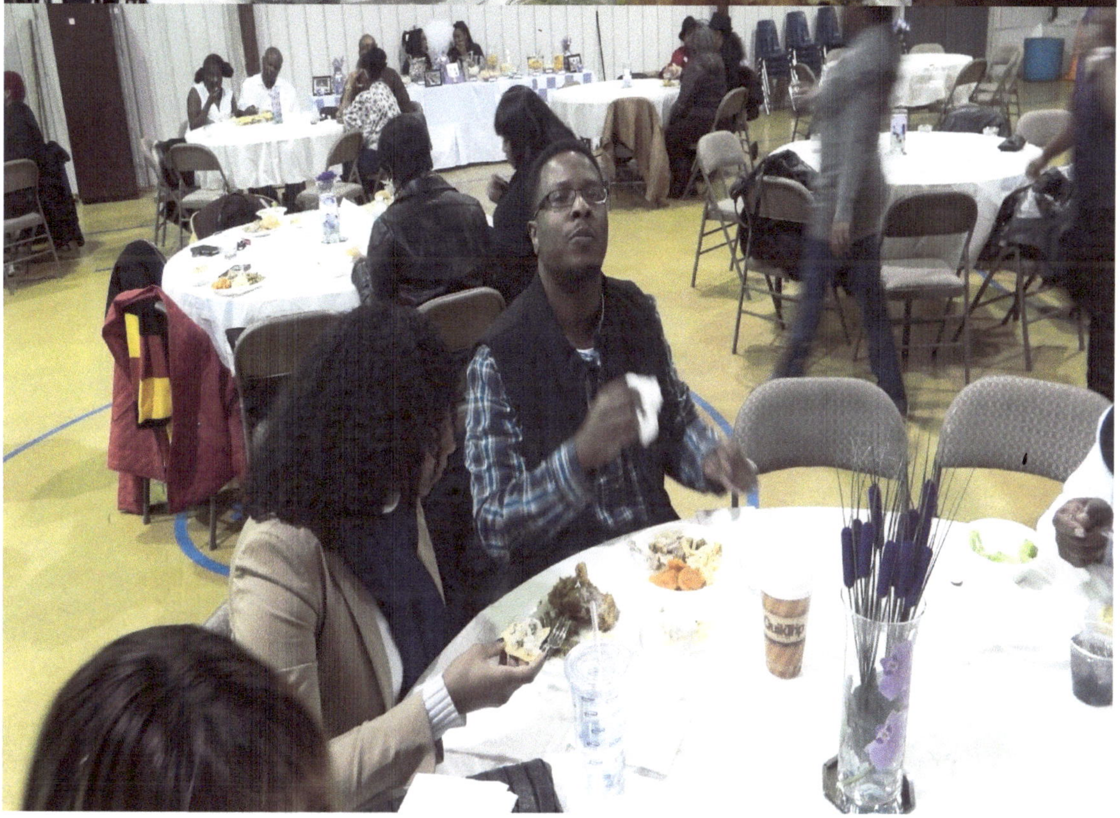

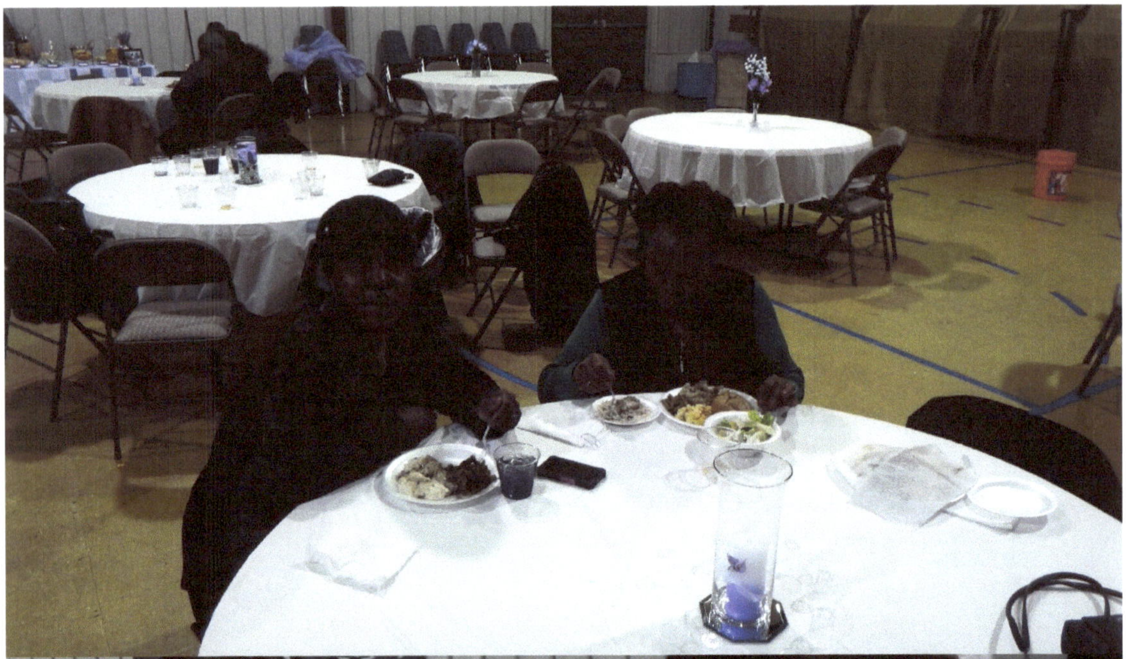

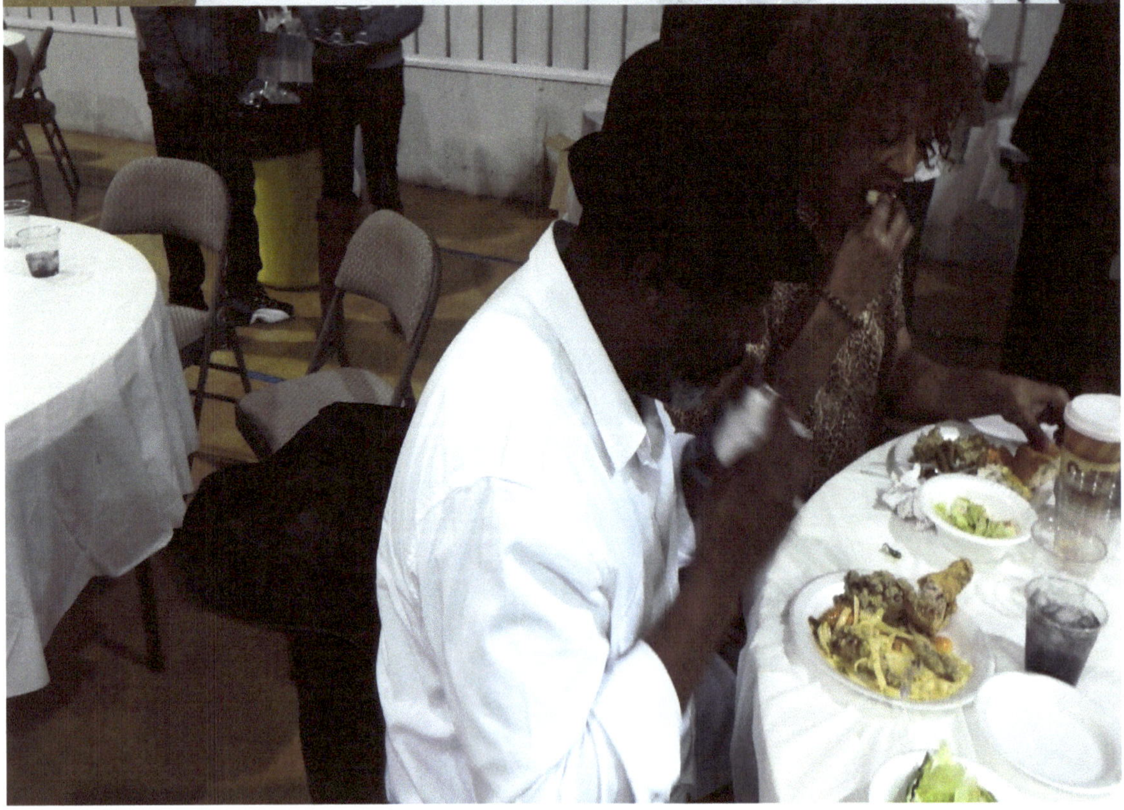

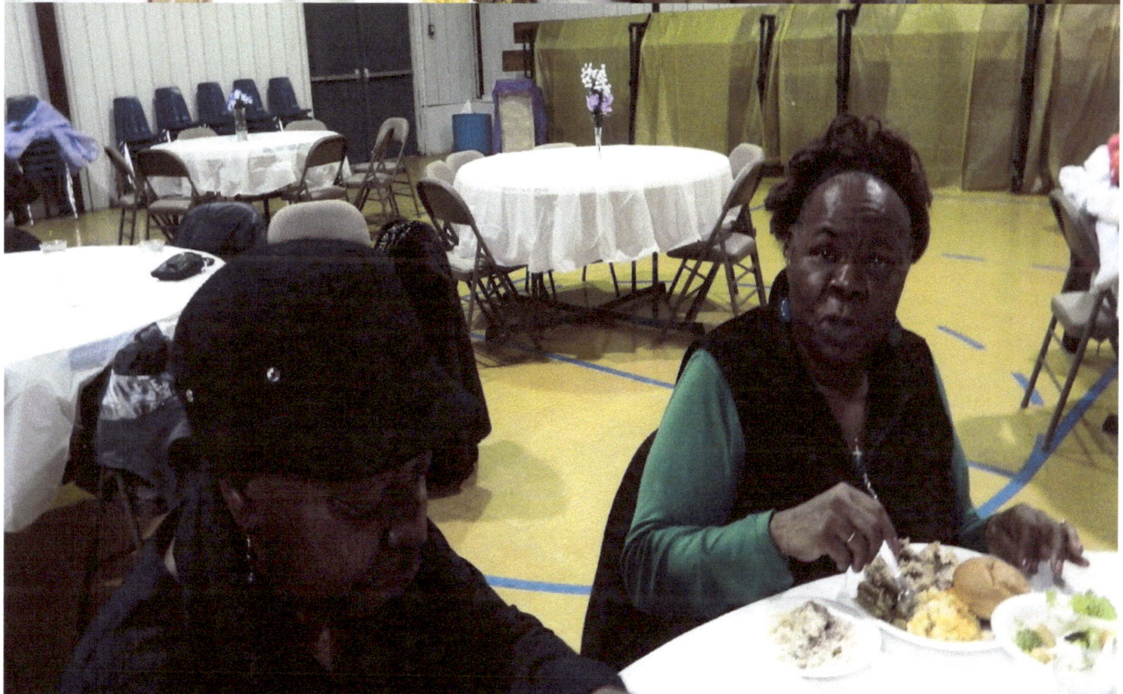

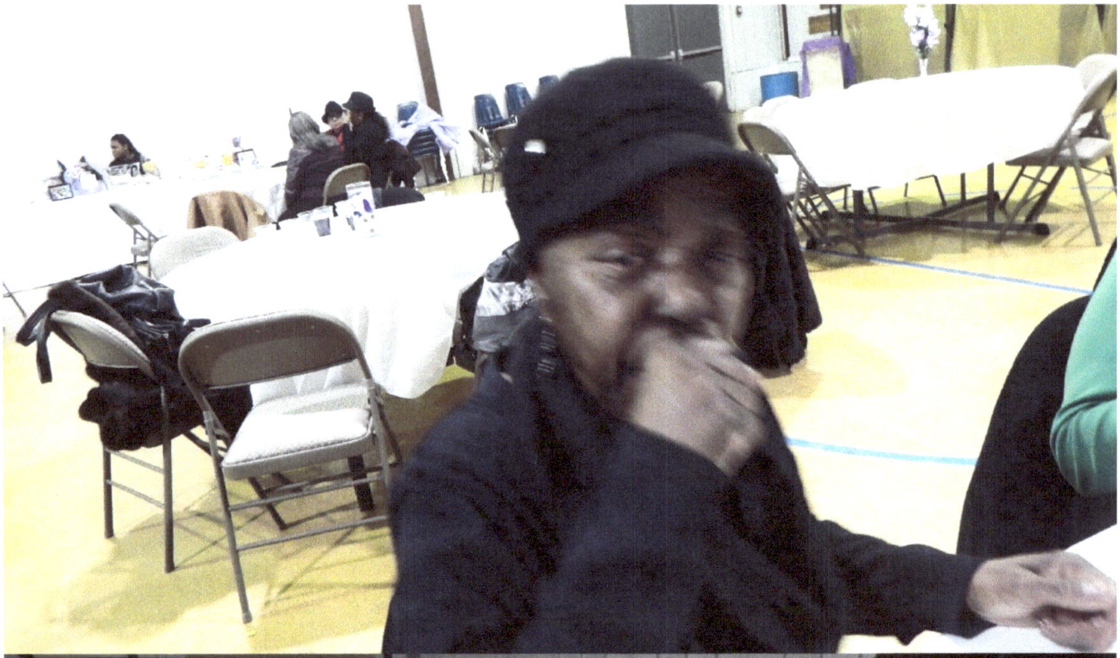

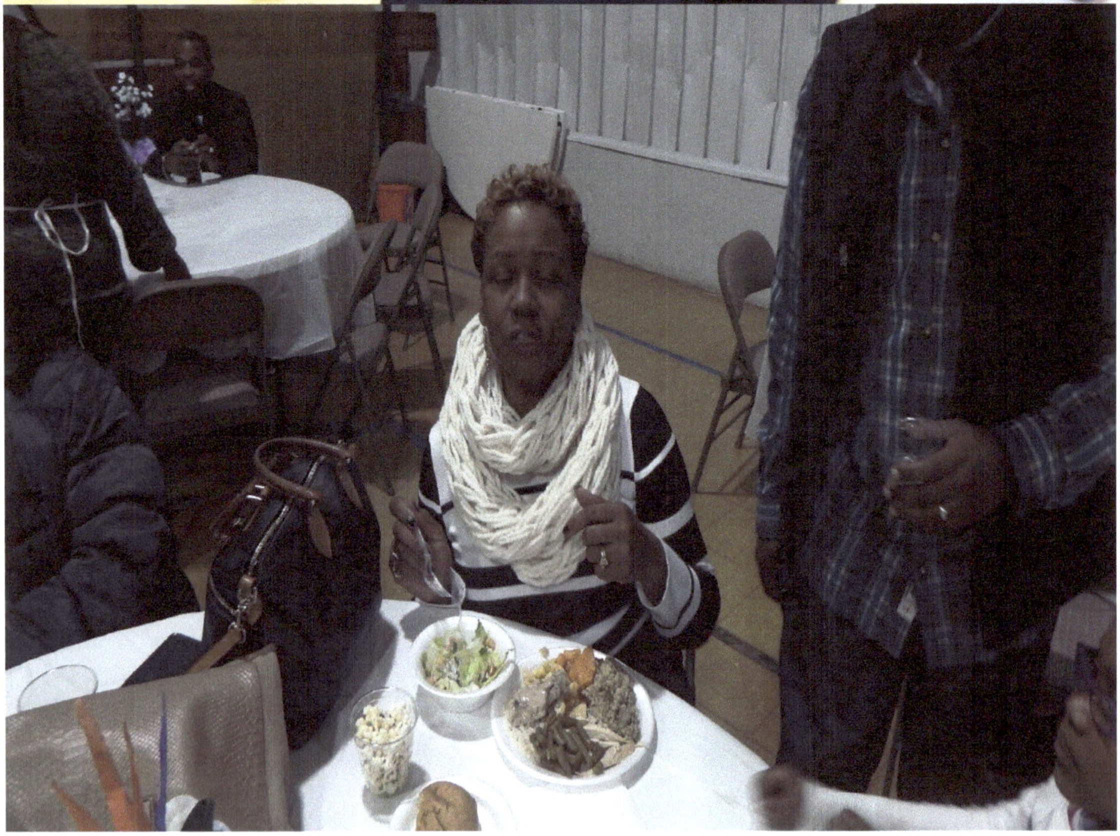

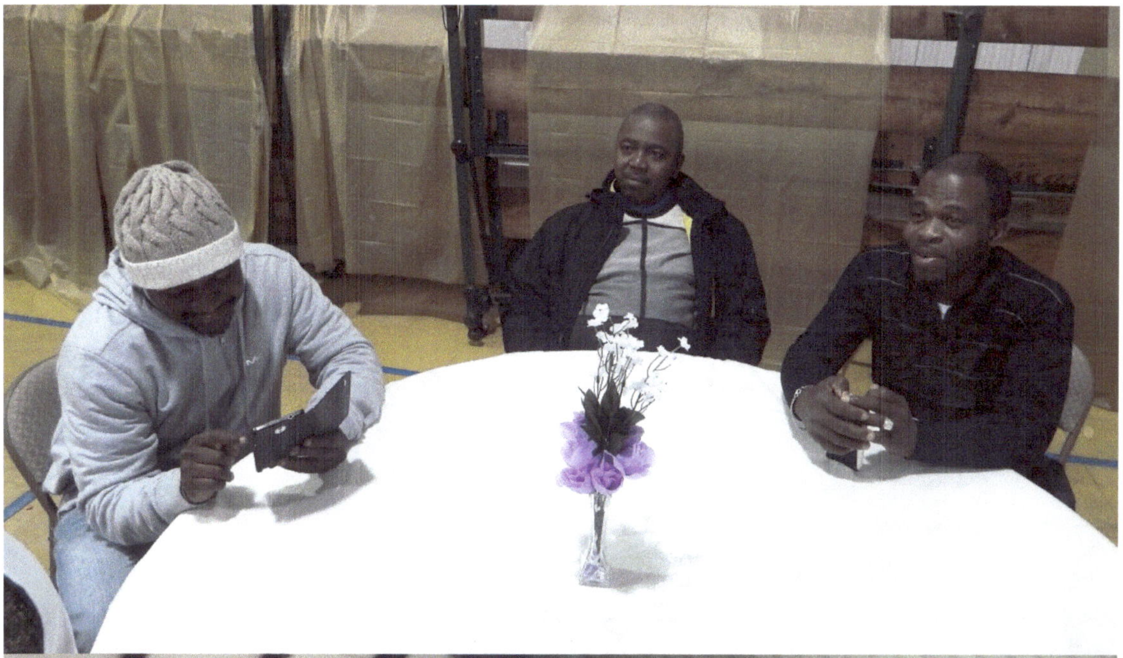

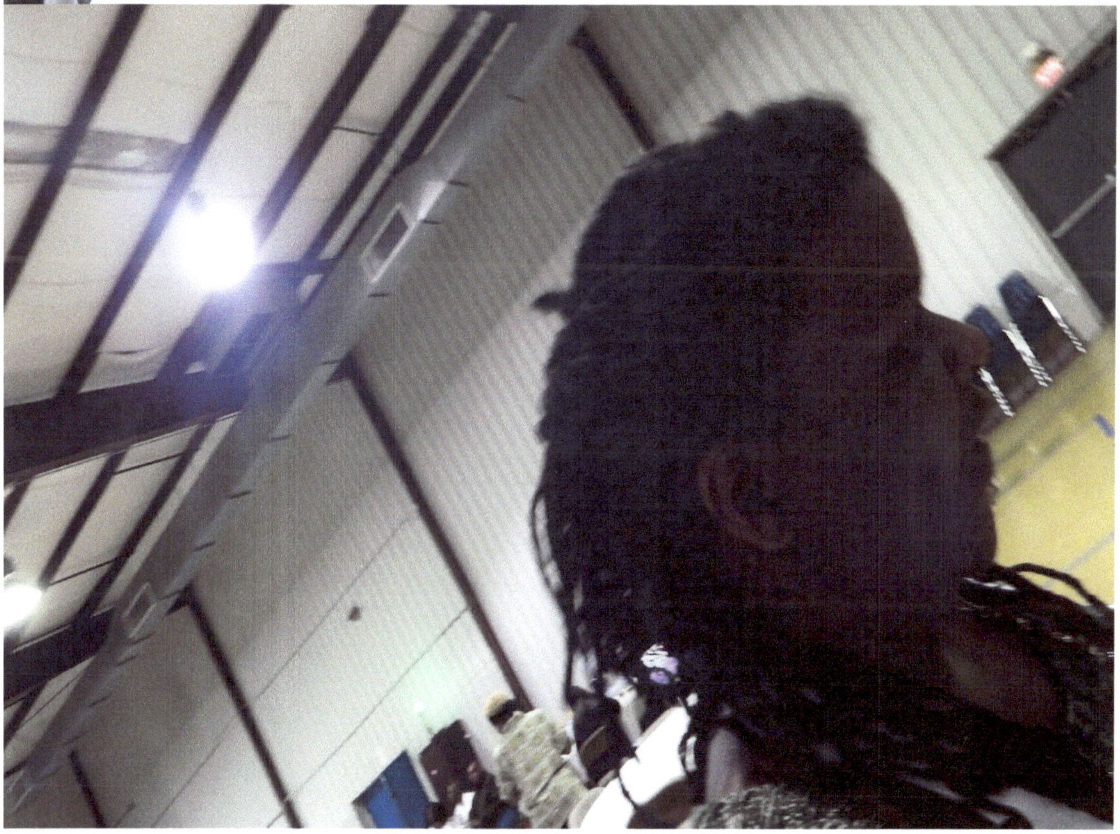

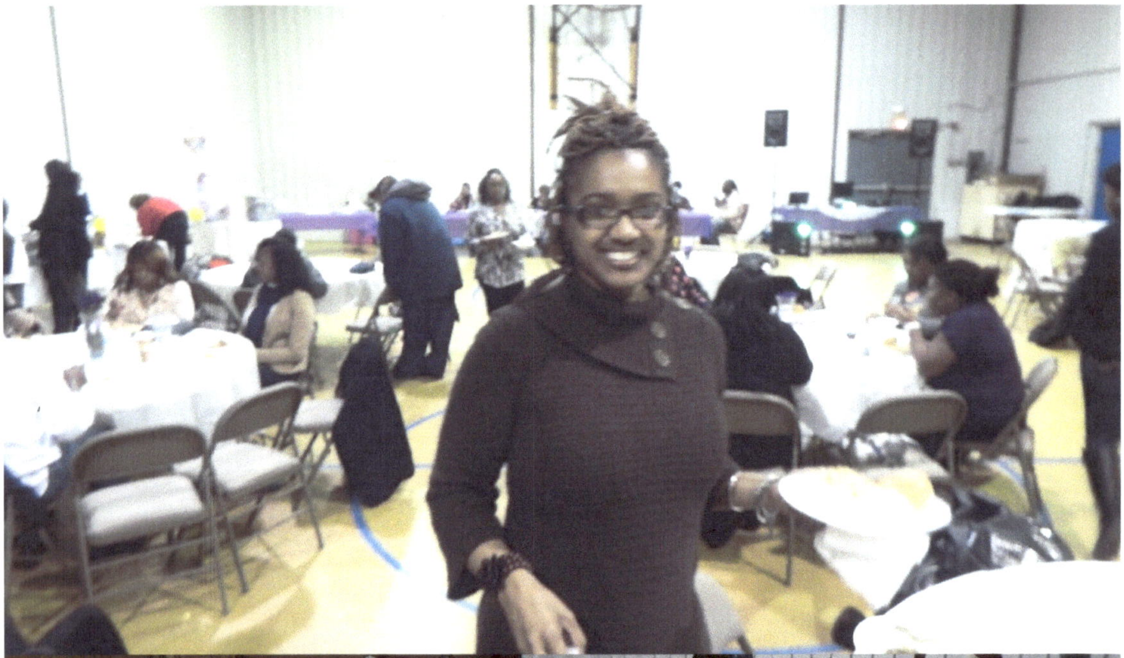

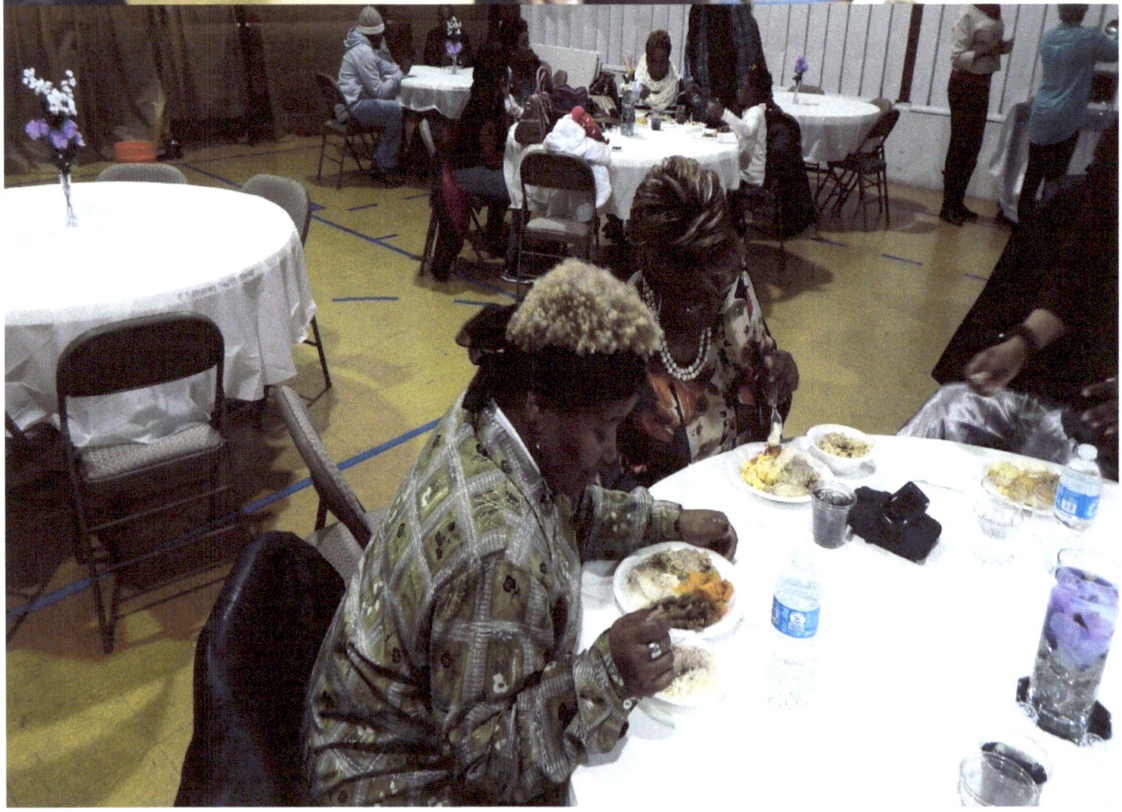

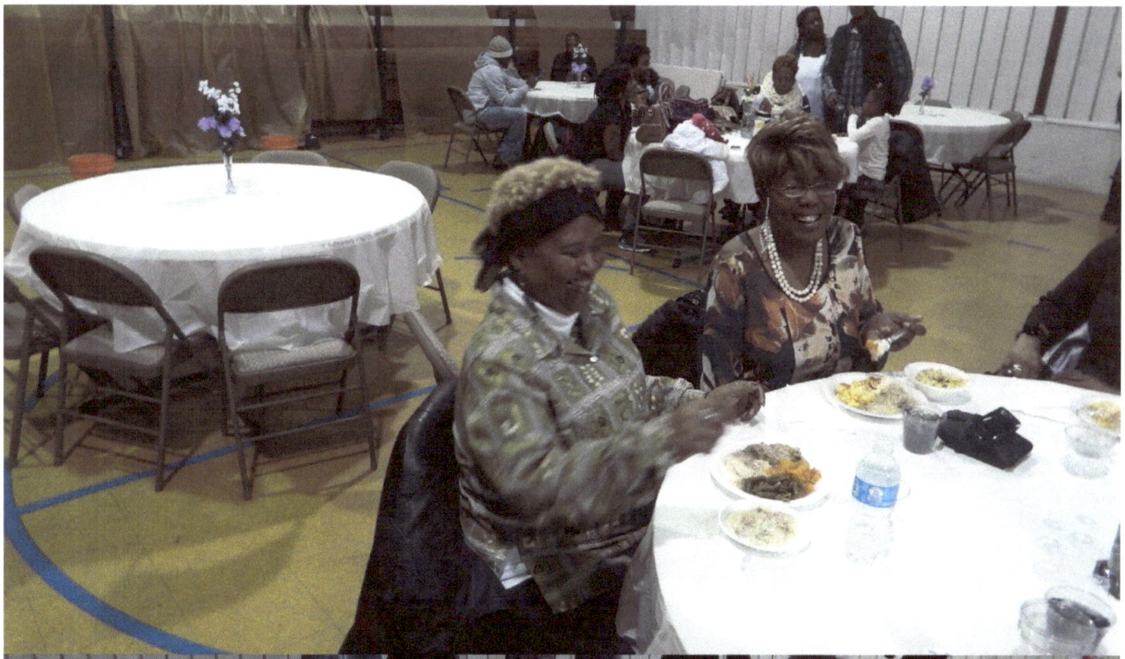
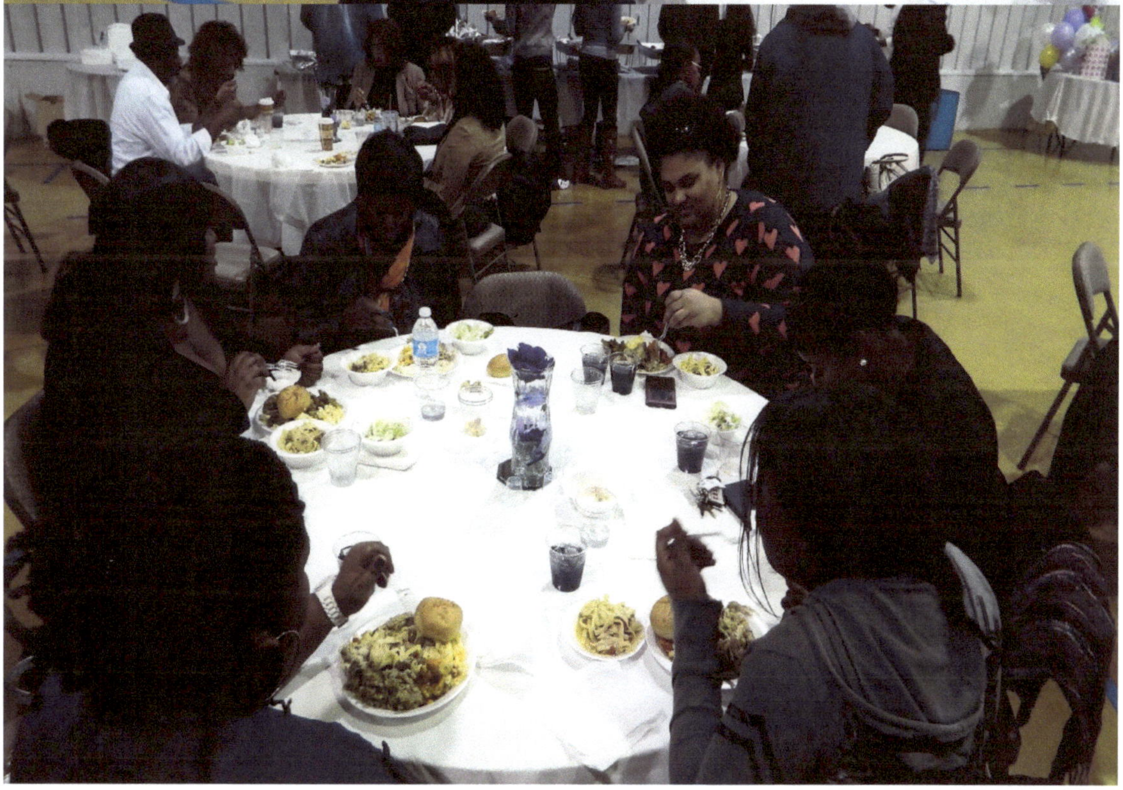

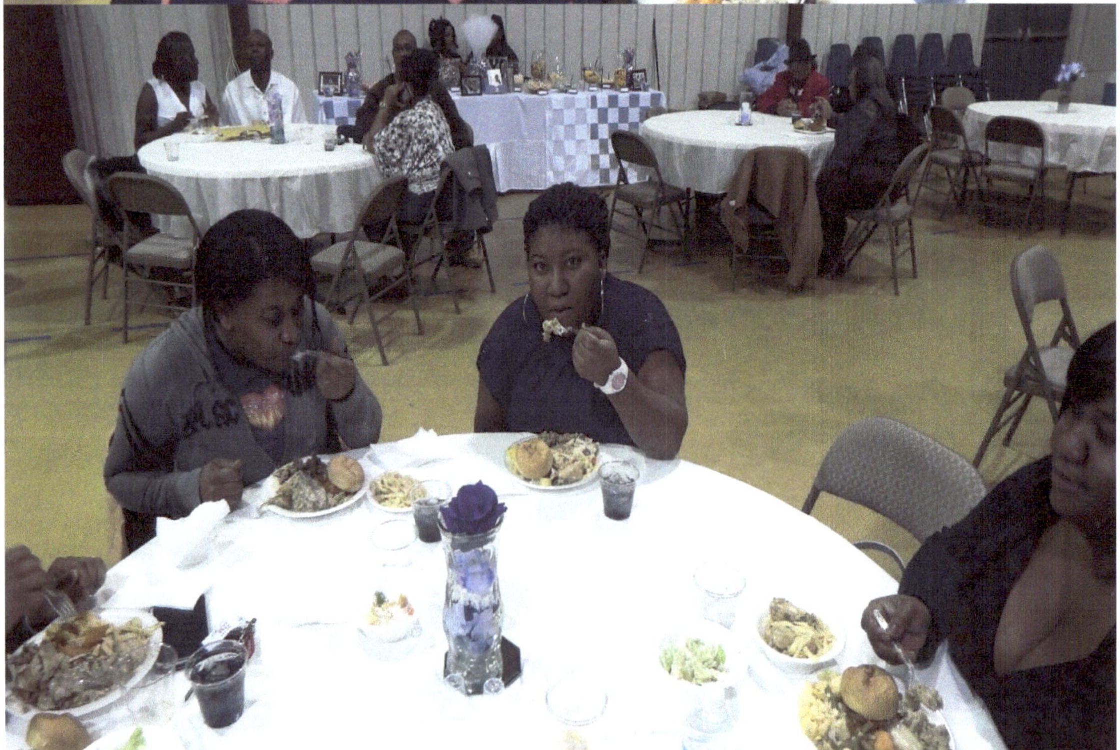

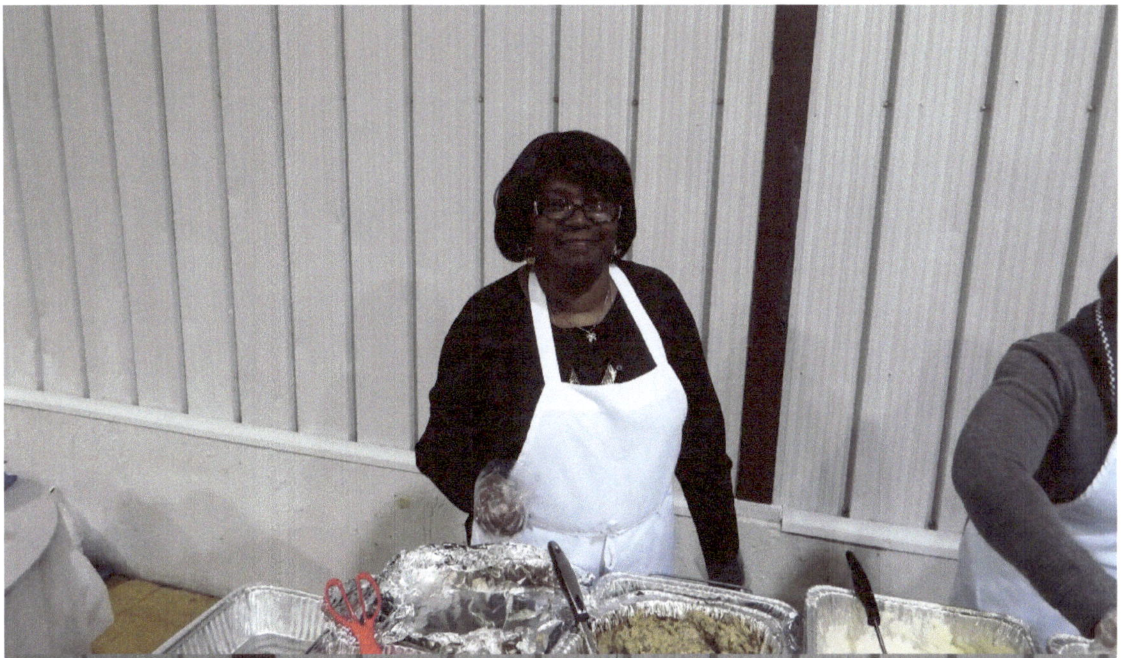
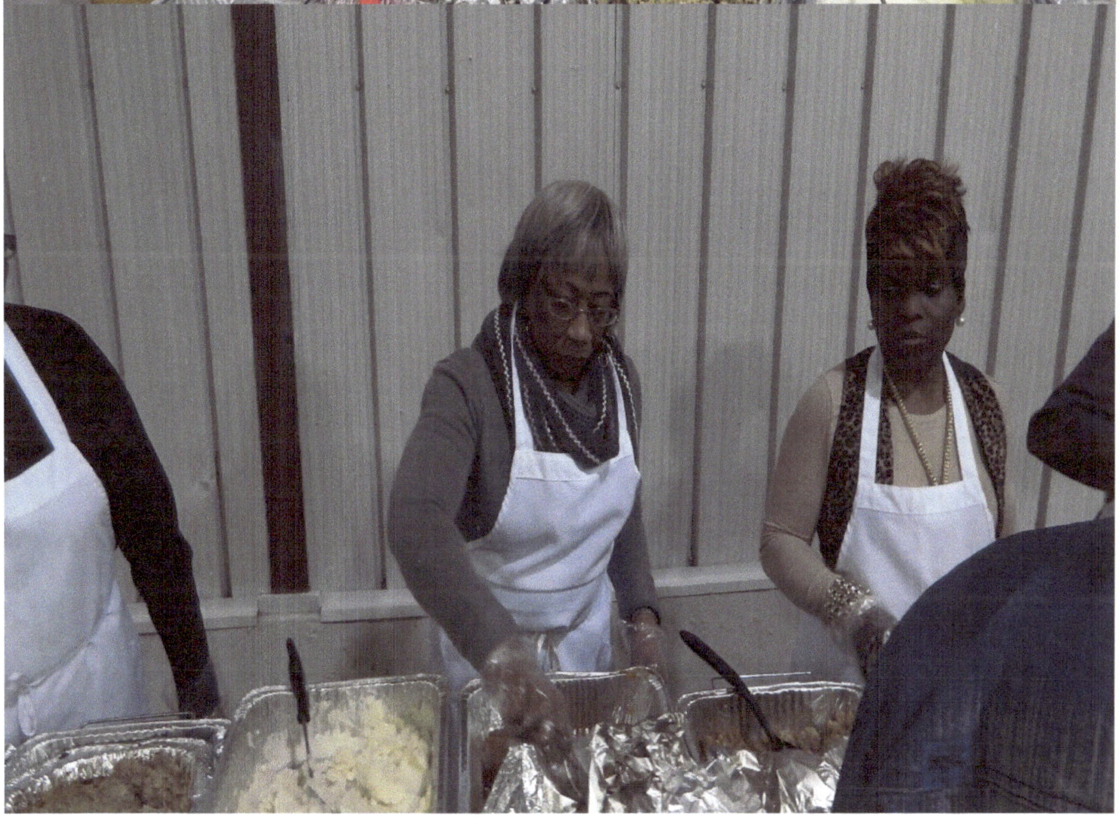

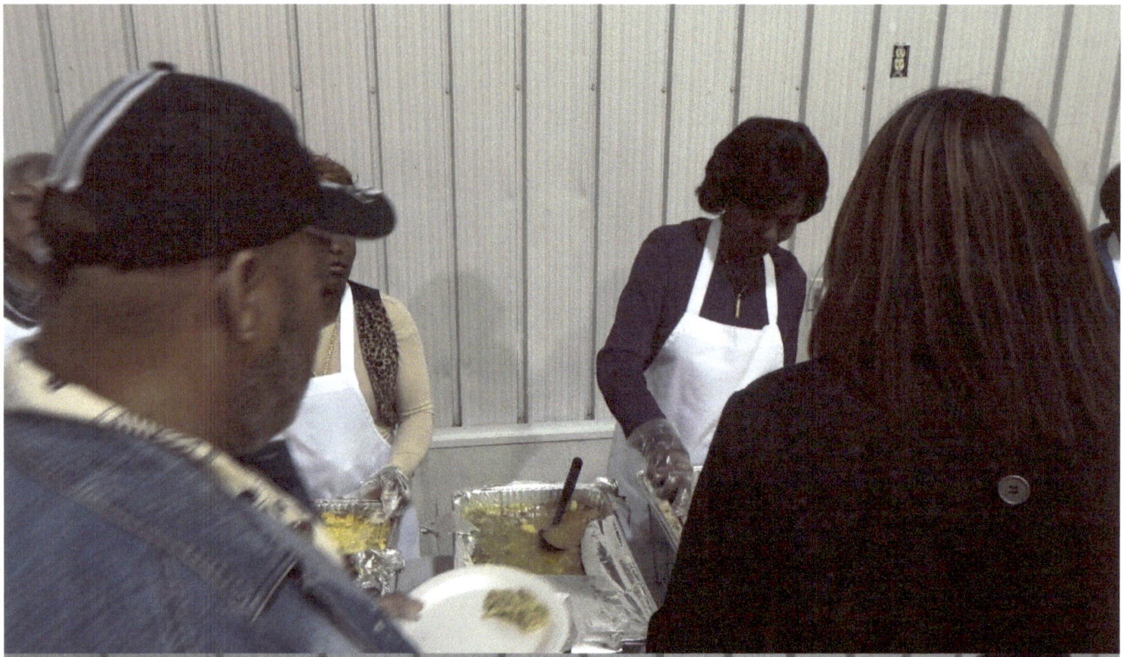

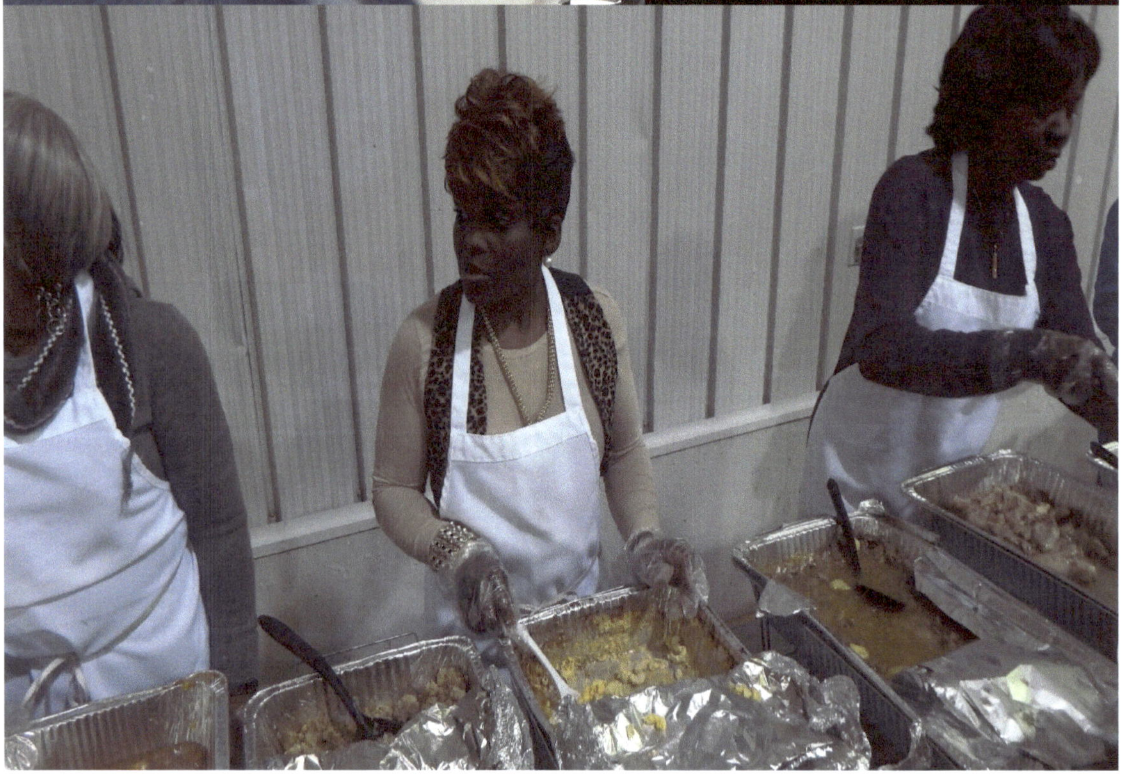

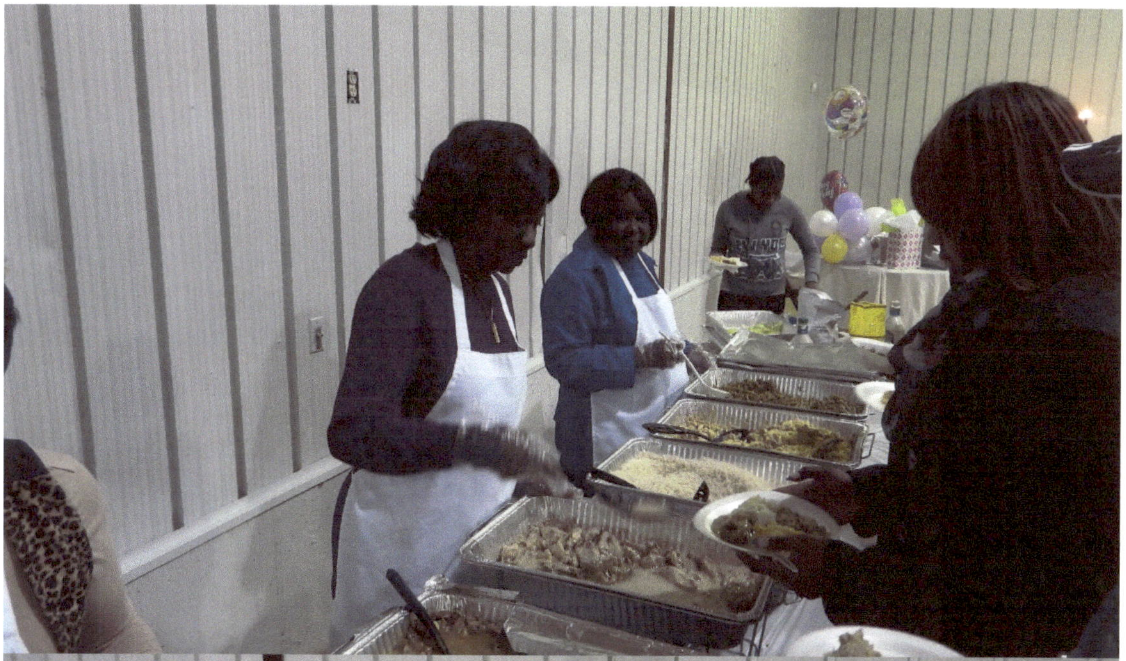

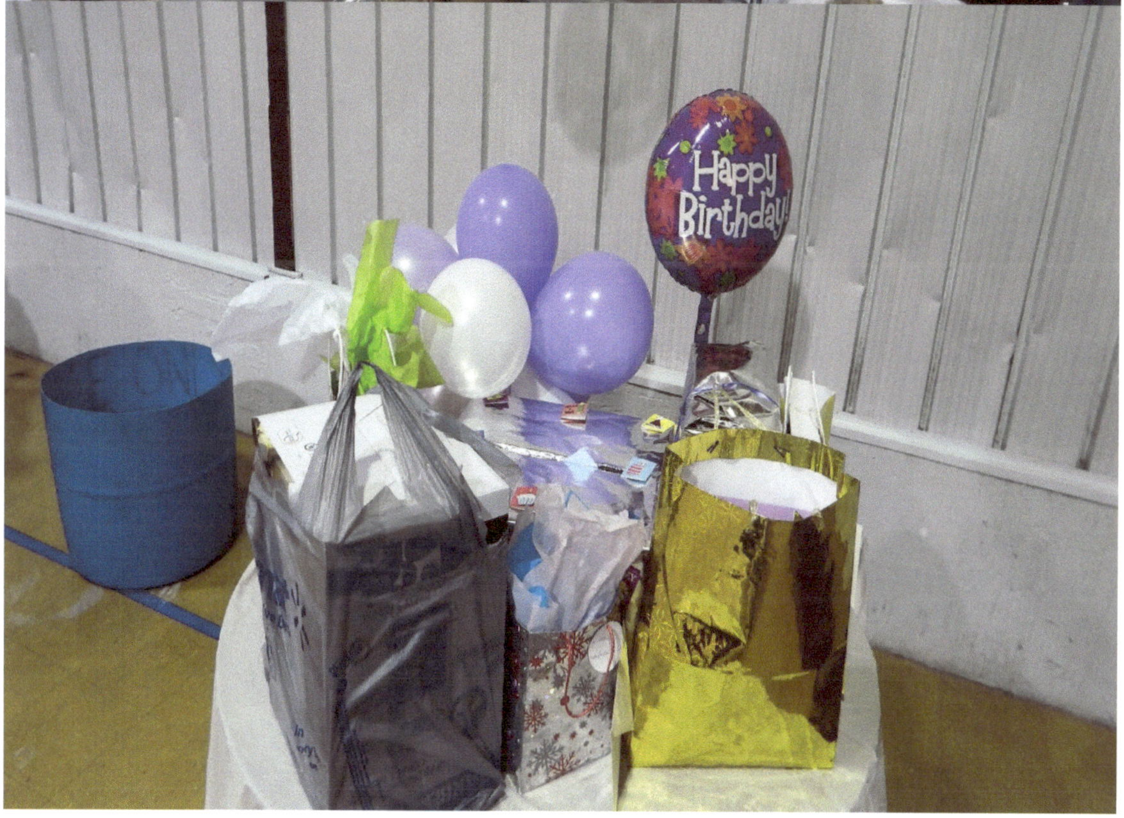
Happy Birthday!

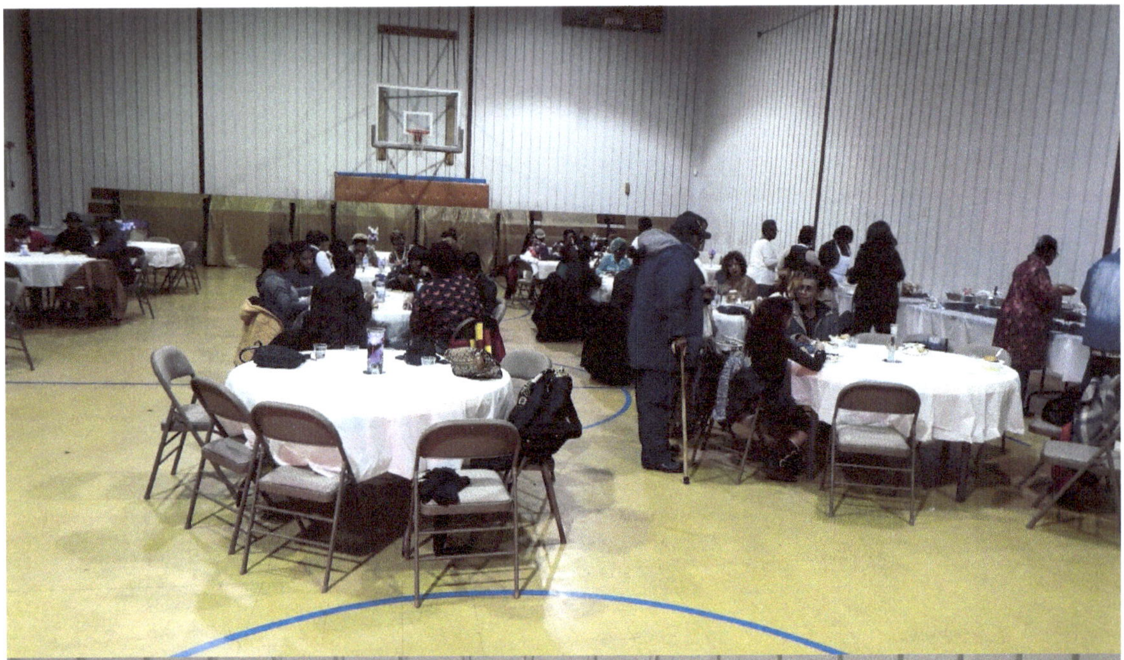

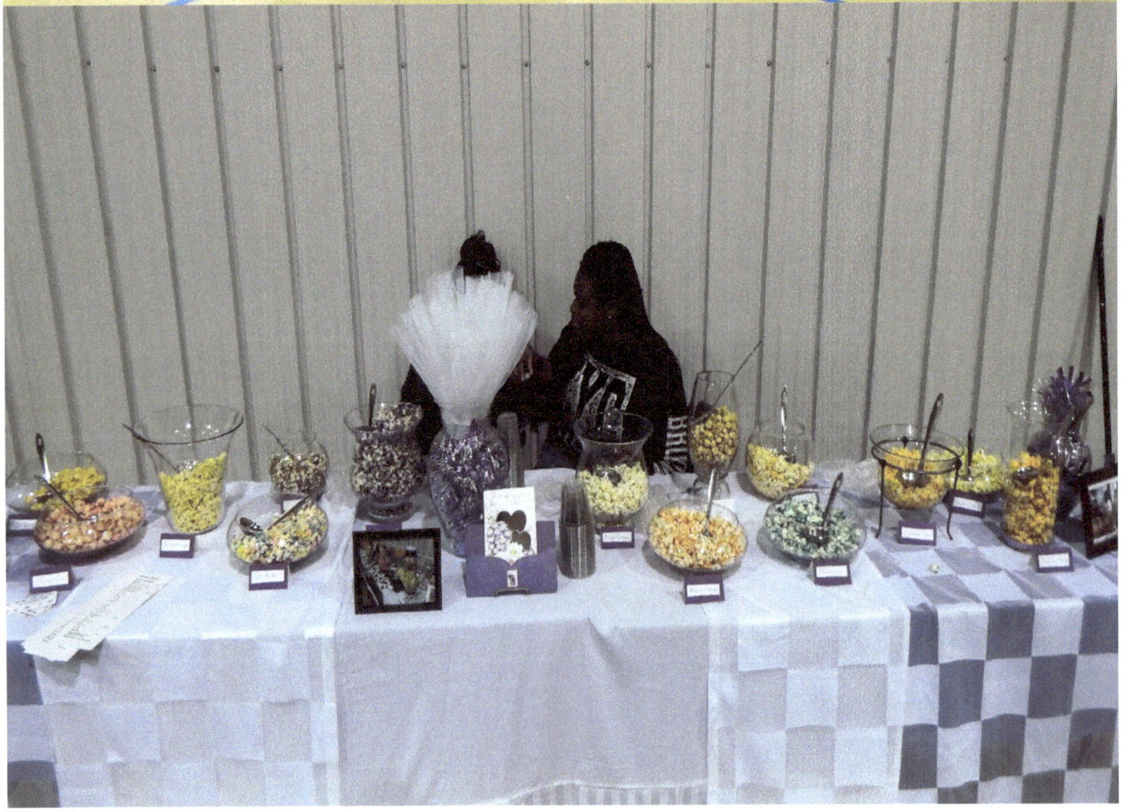

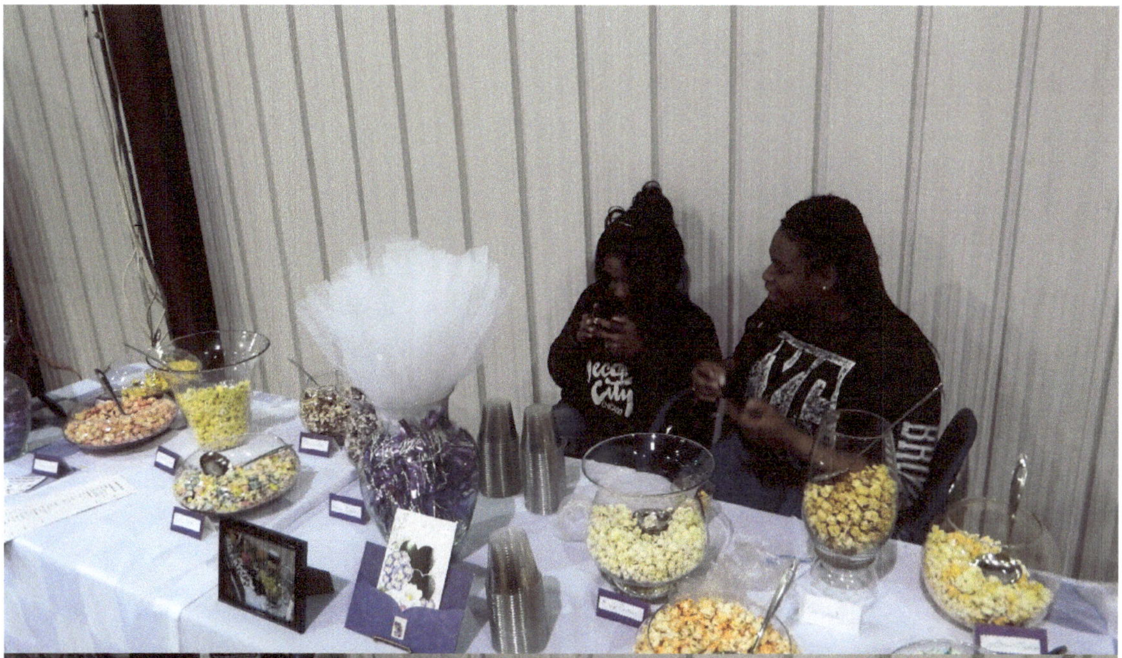

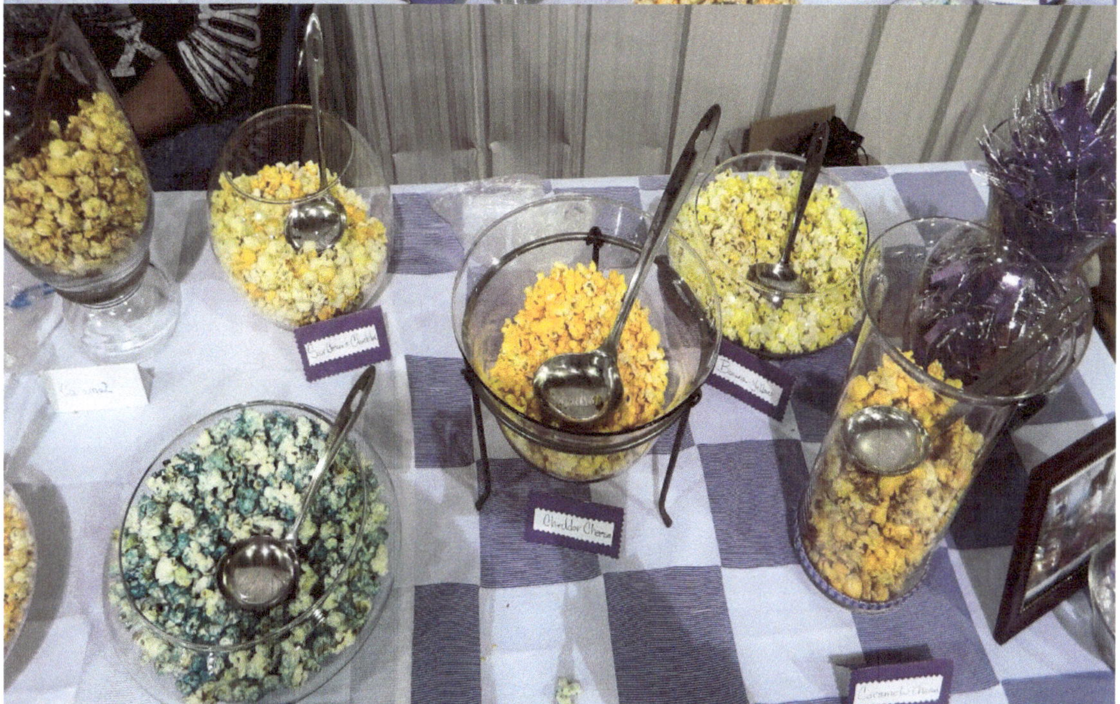
Cheddar Cheese
Blueberry

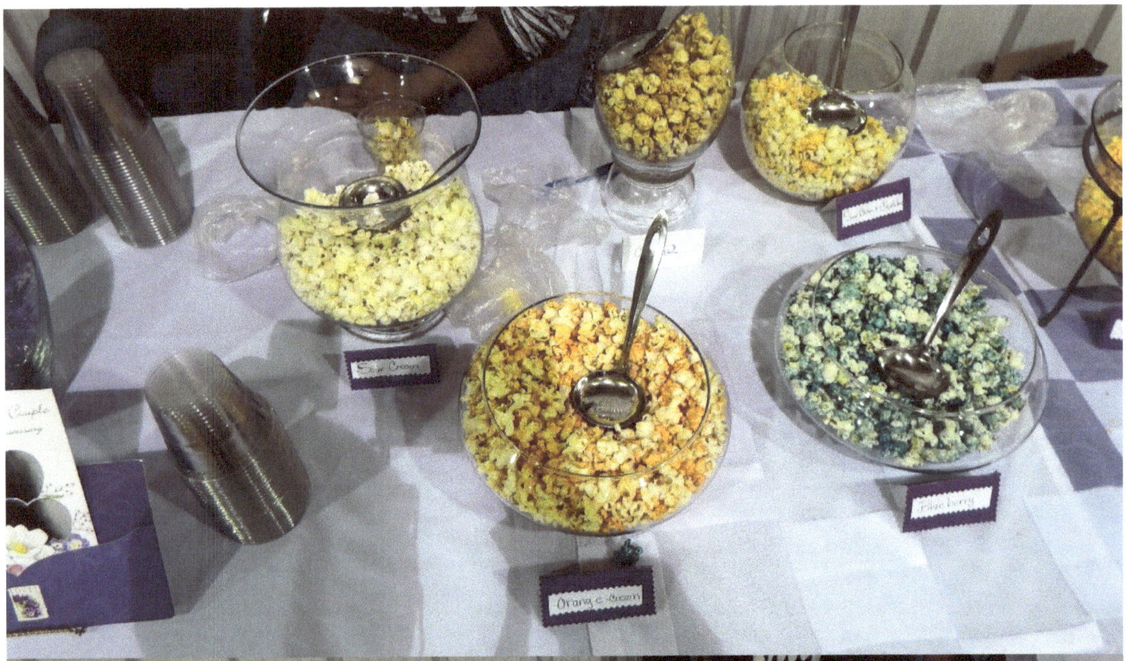
Orange-cream
Blueberry

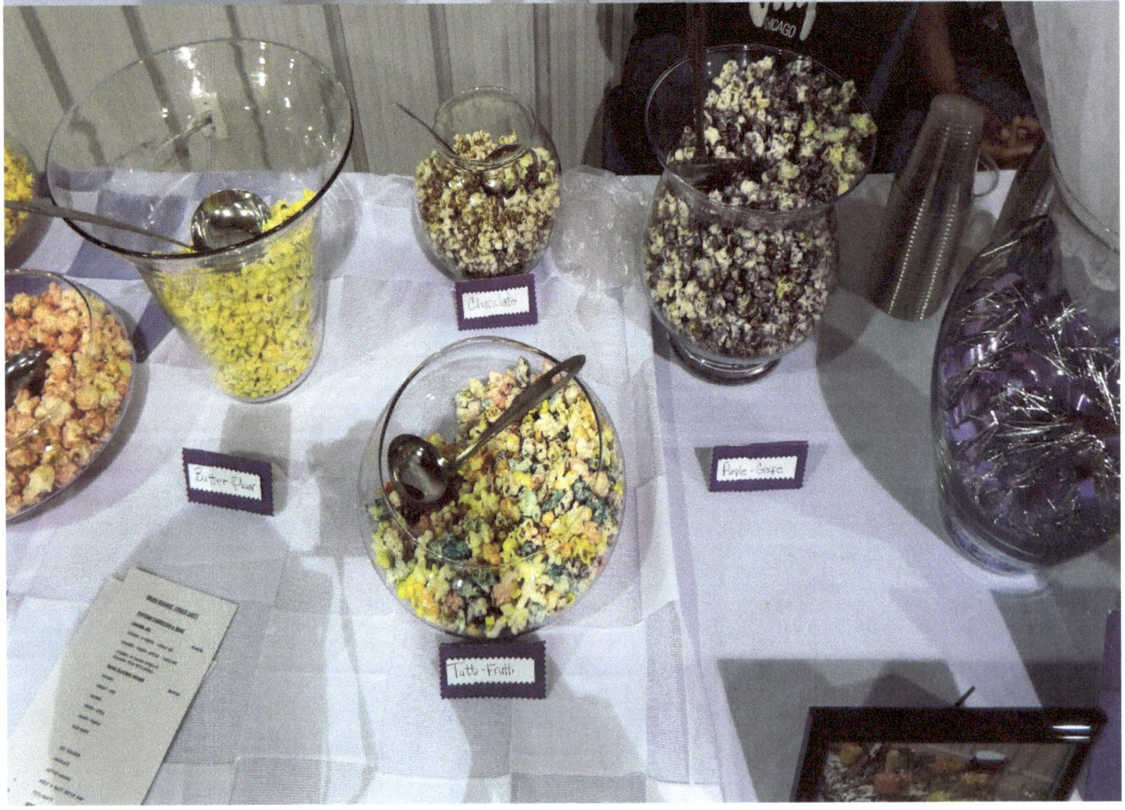
CHICAGO
Chocolate
Butter Pecan
Purple-Grape
Tutti-Frutti

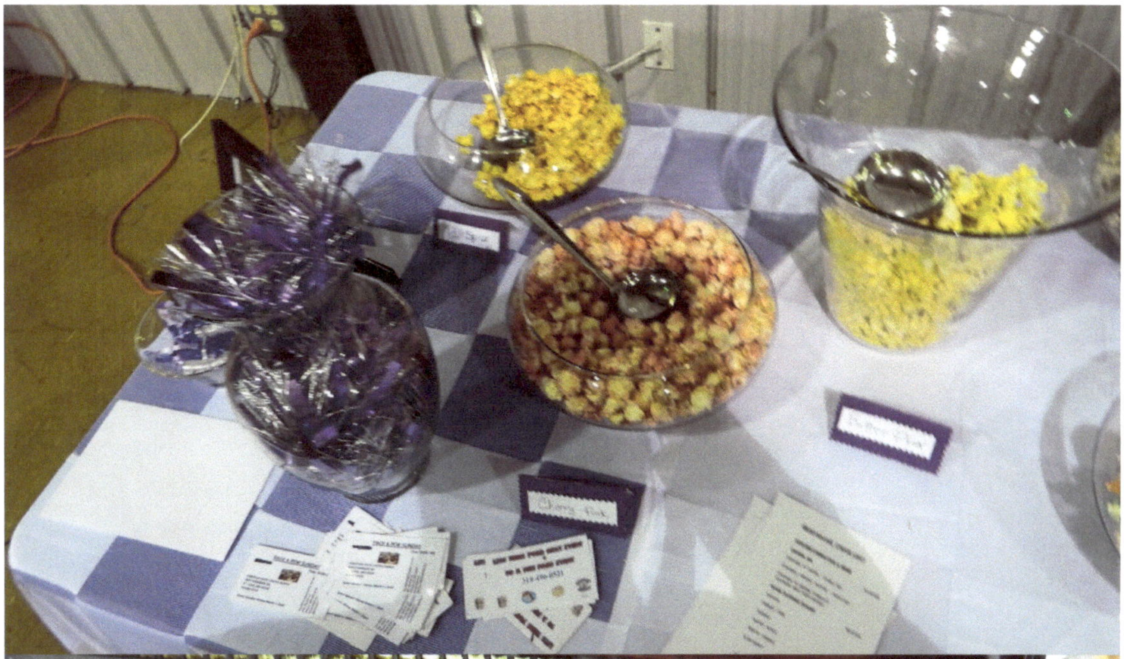

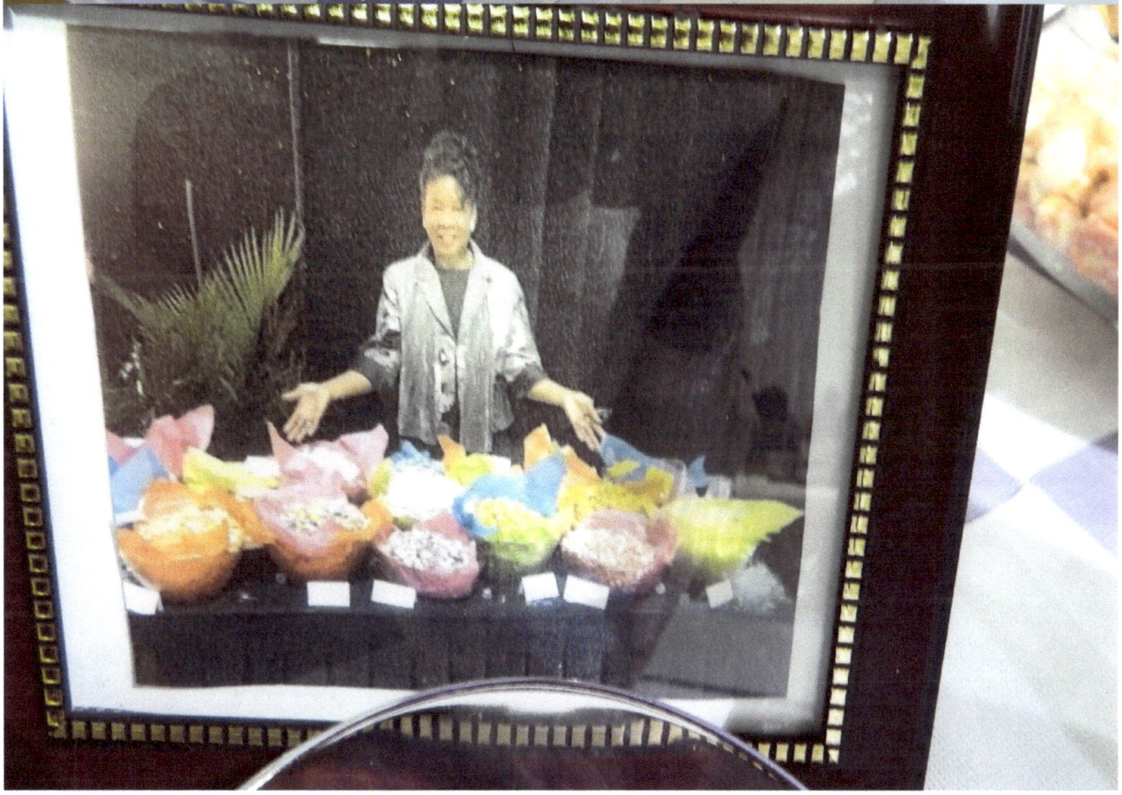

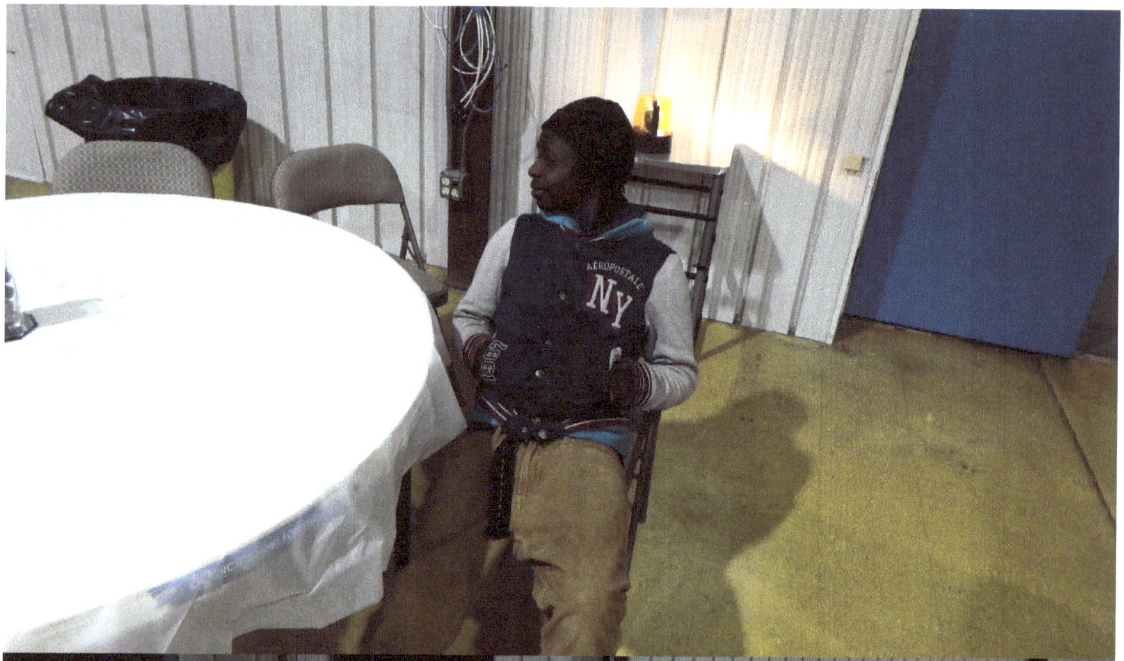
AEROPOSTALE
NY
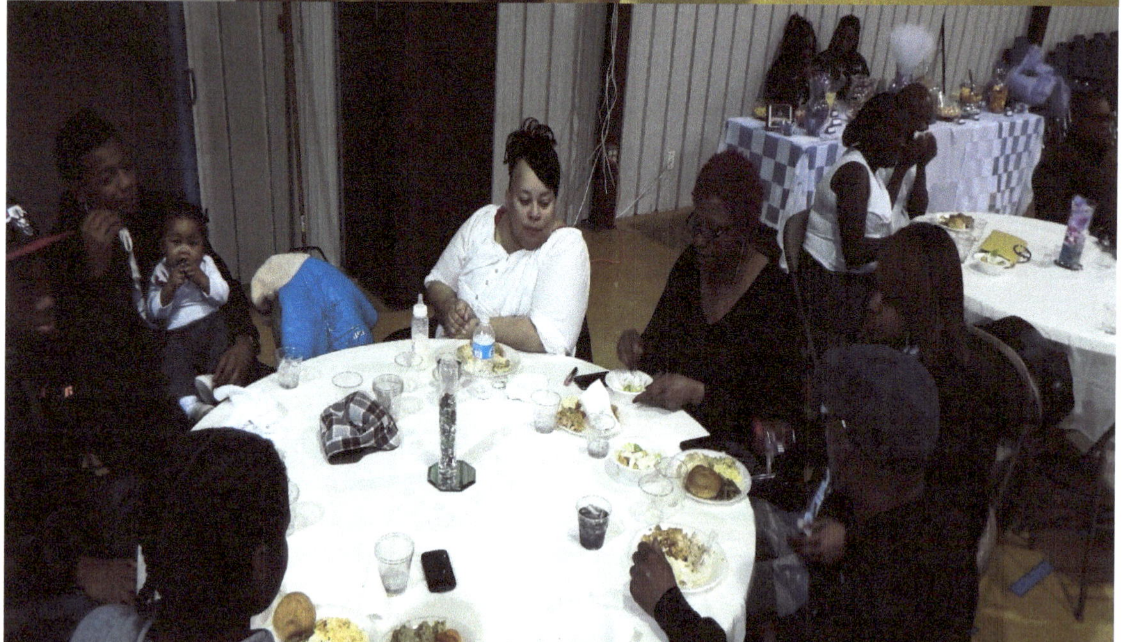

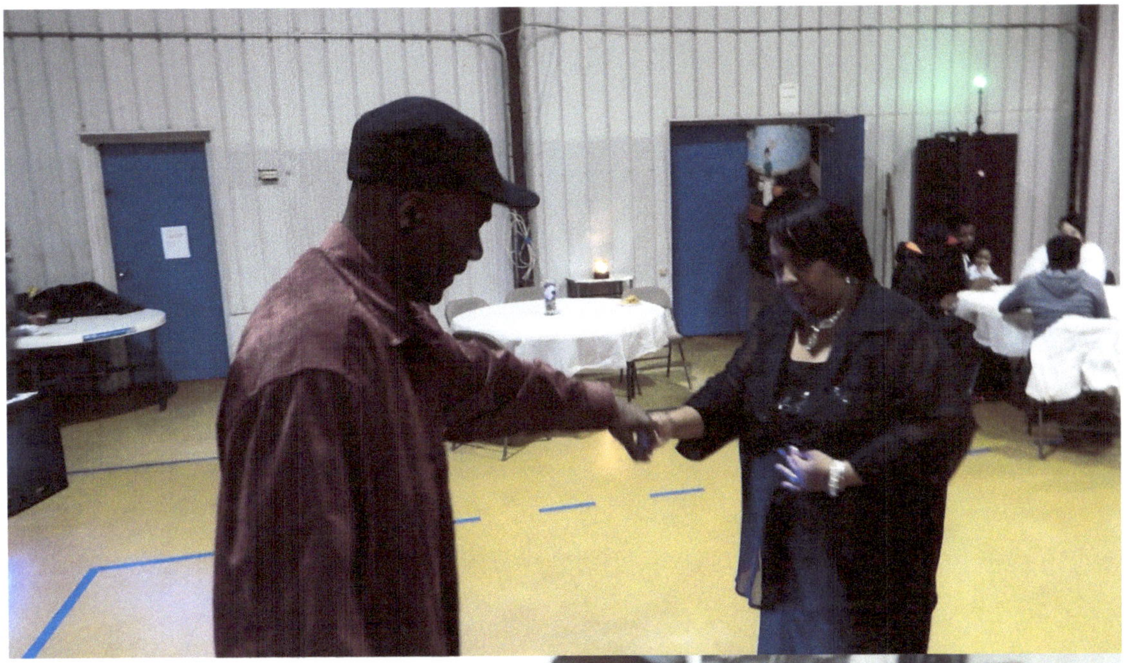

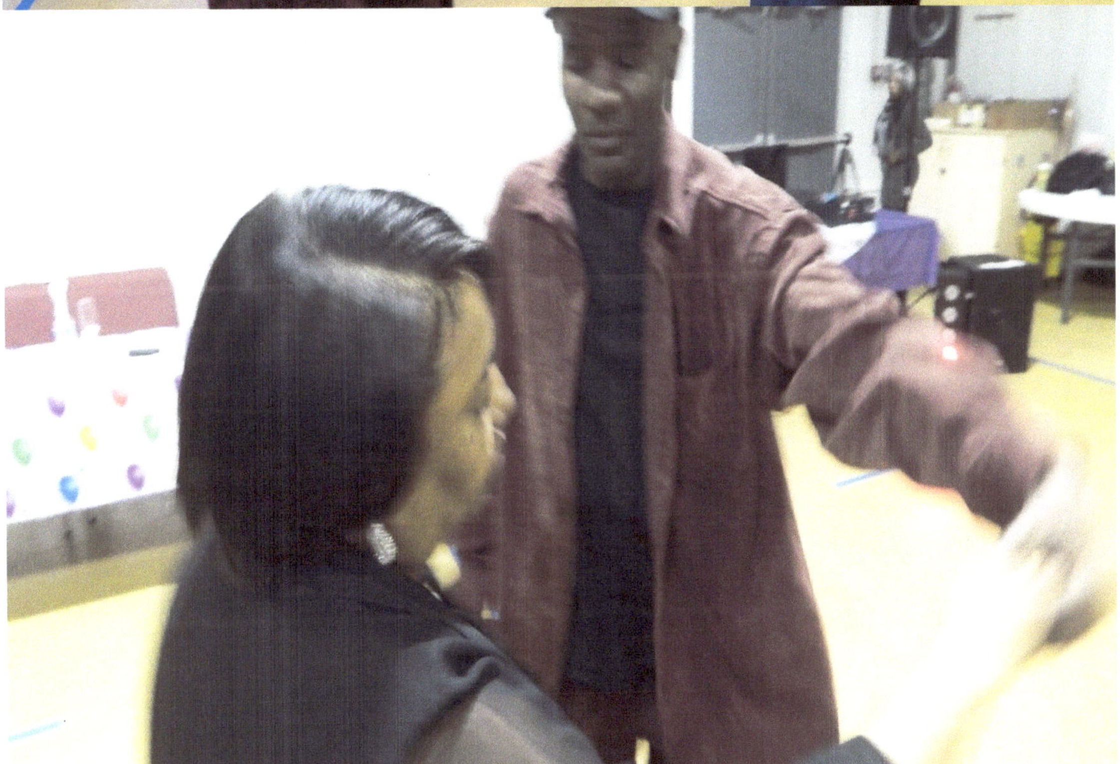

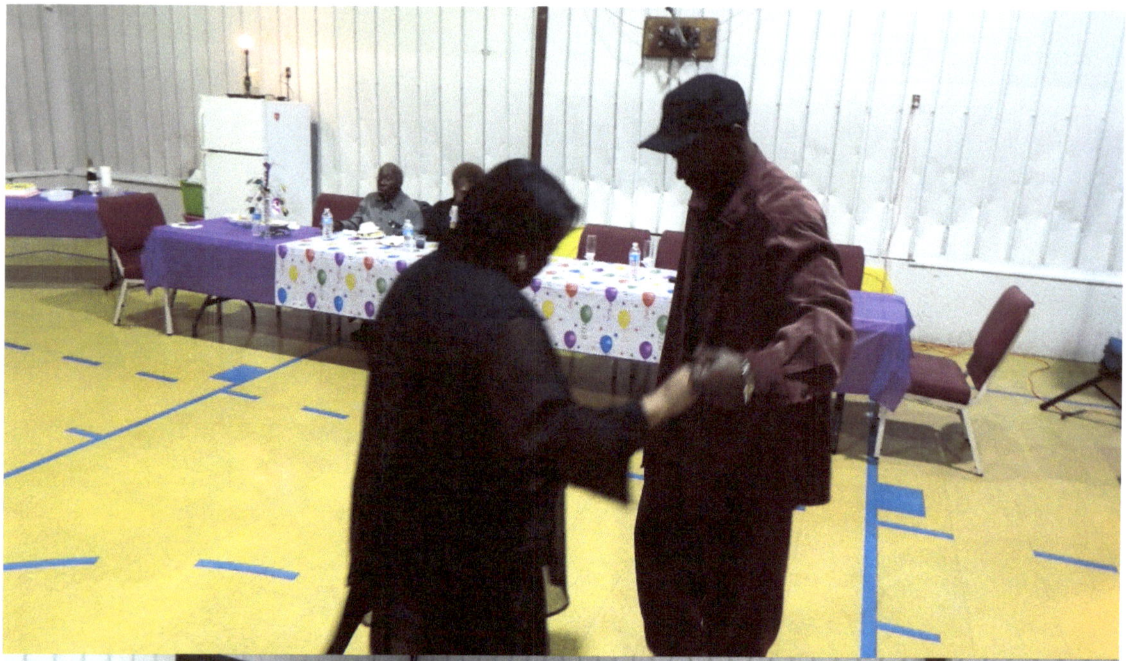

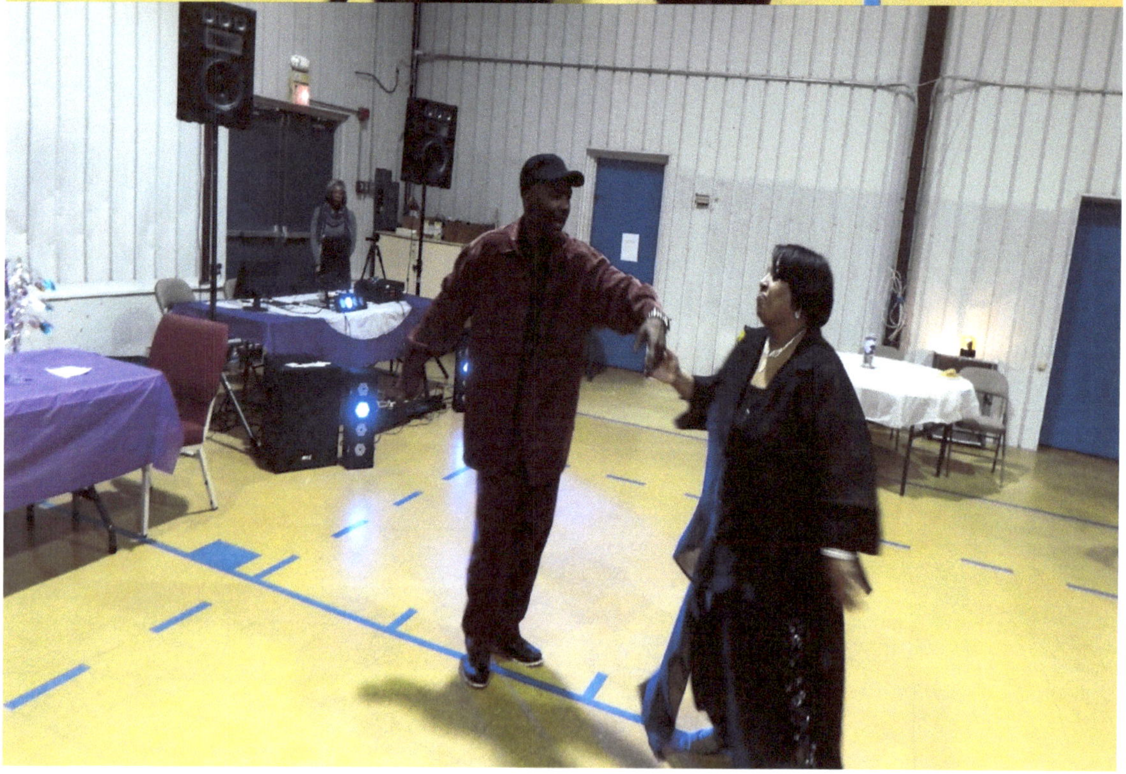

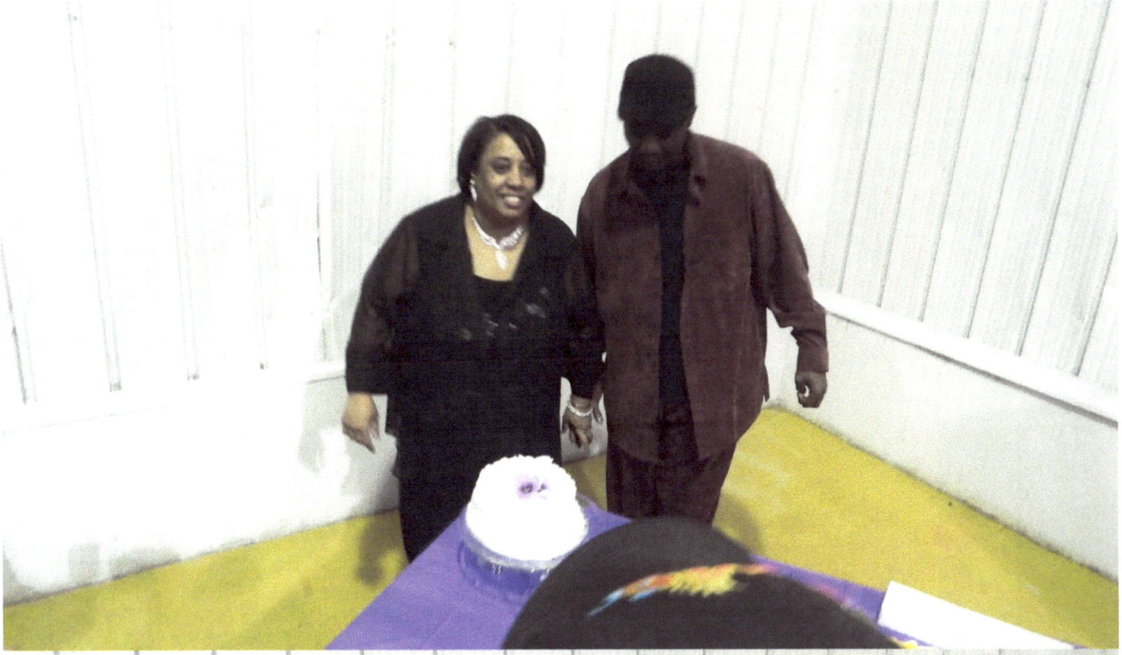

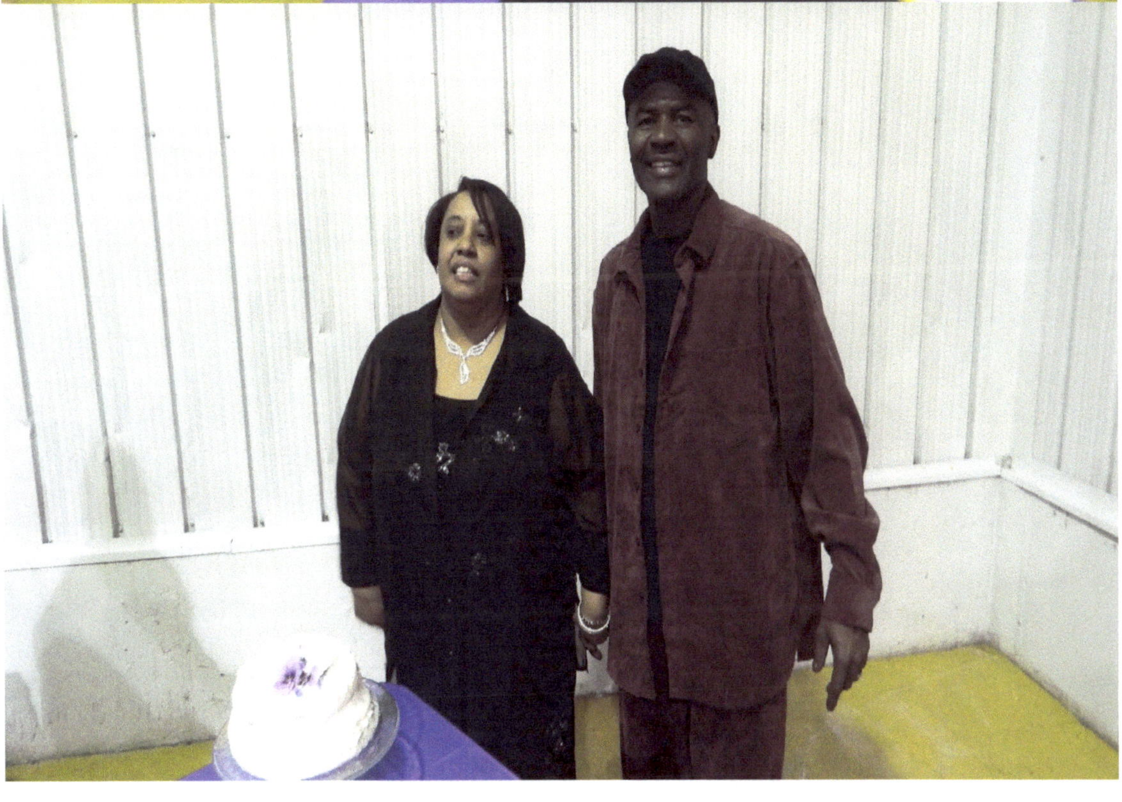

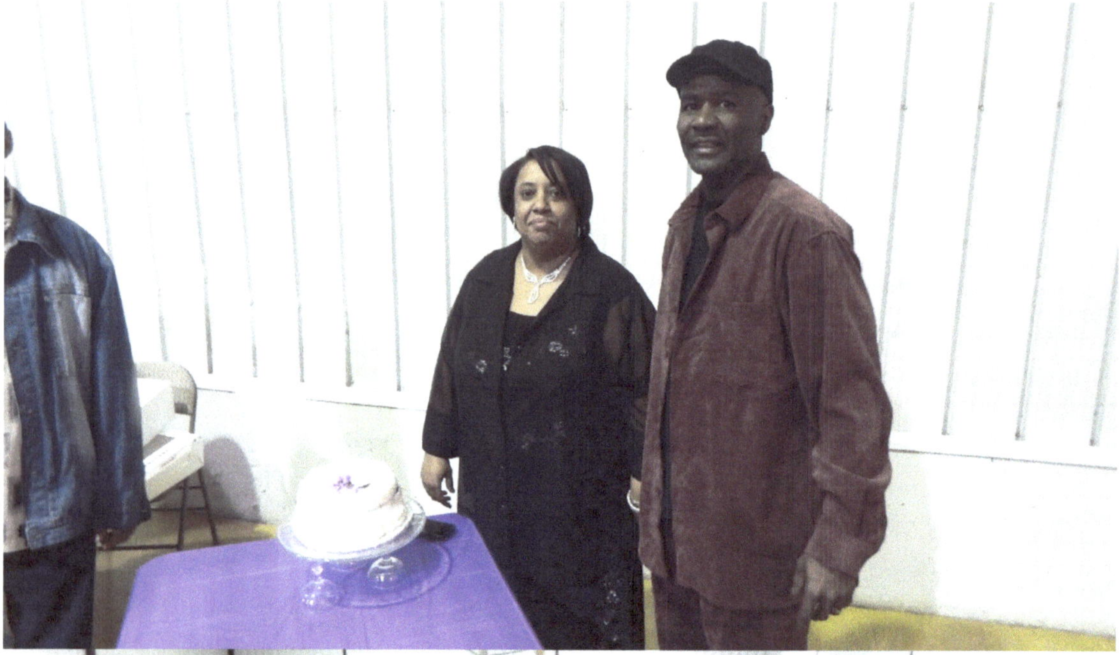

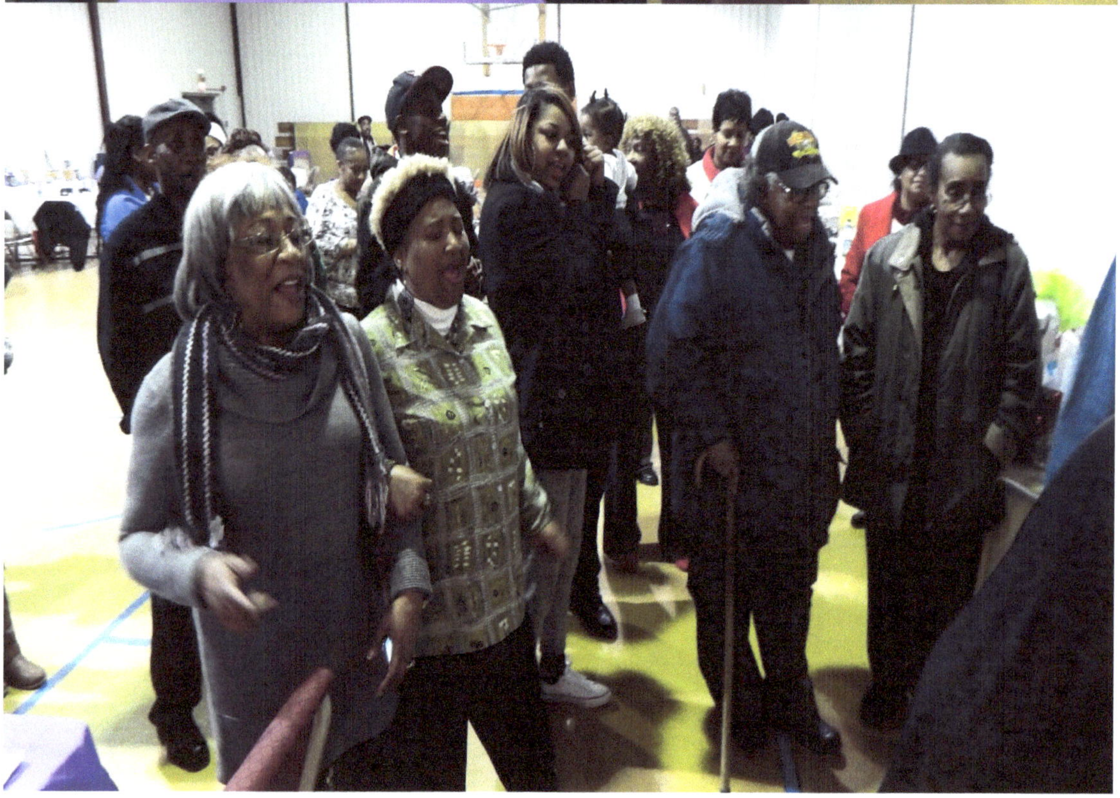

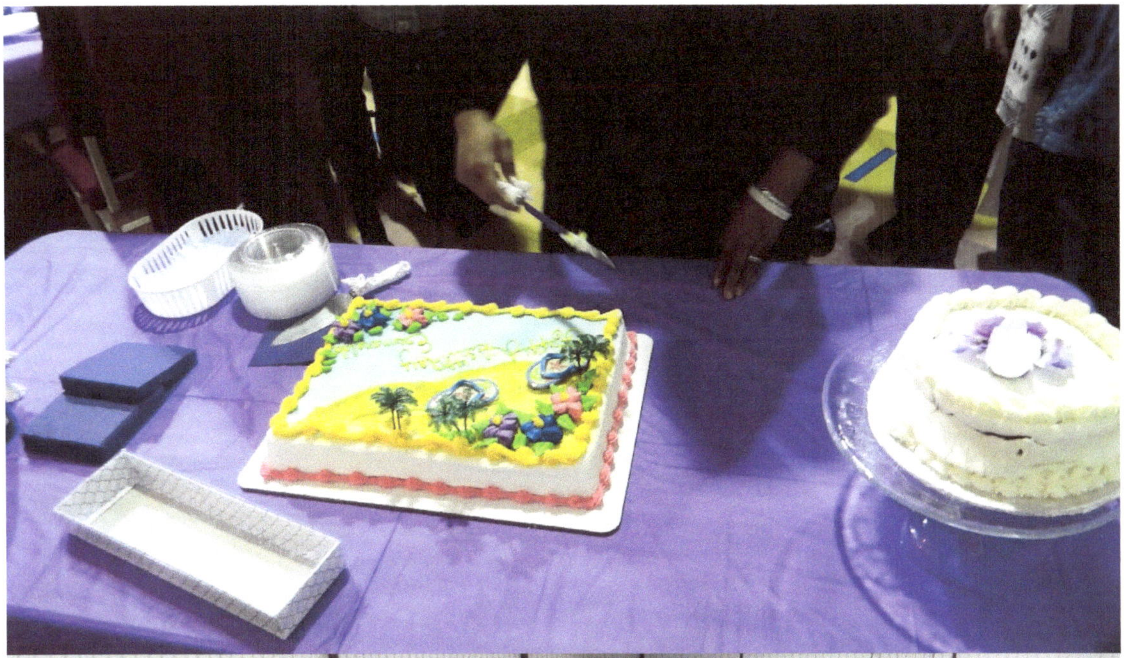

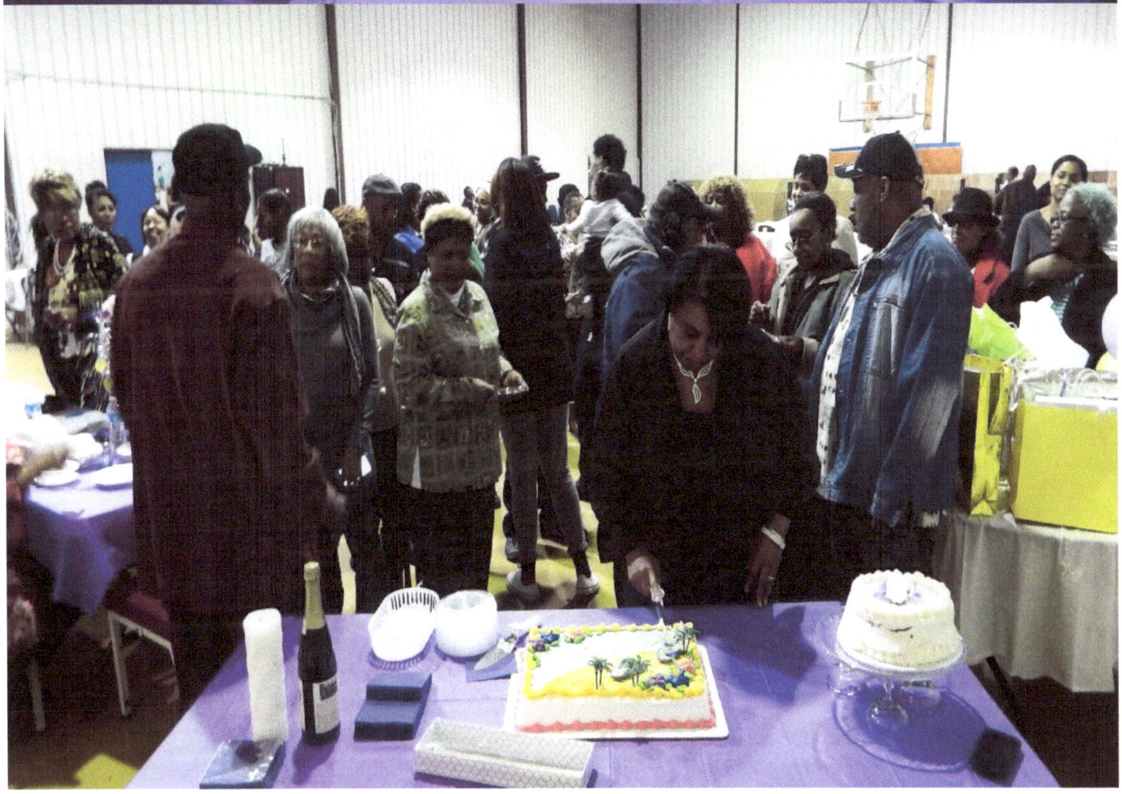

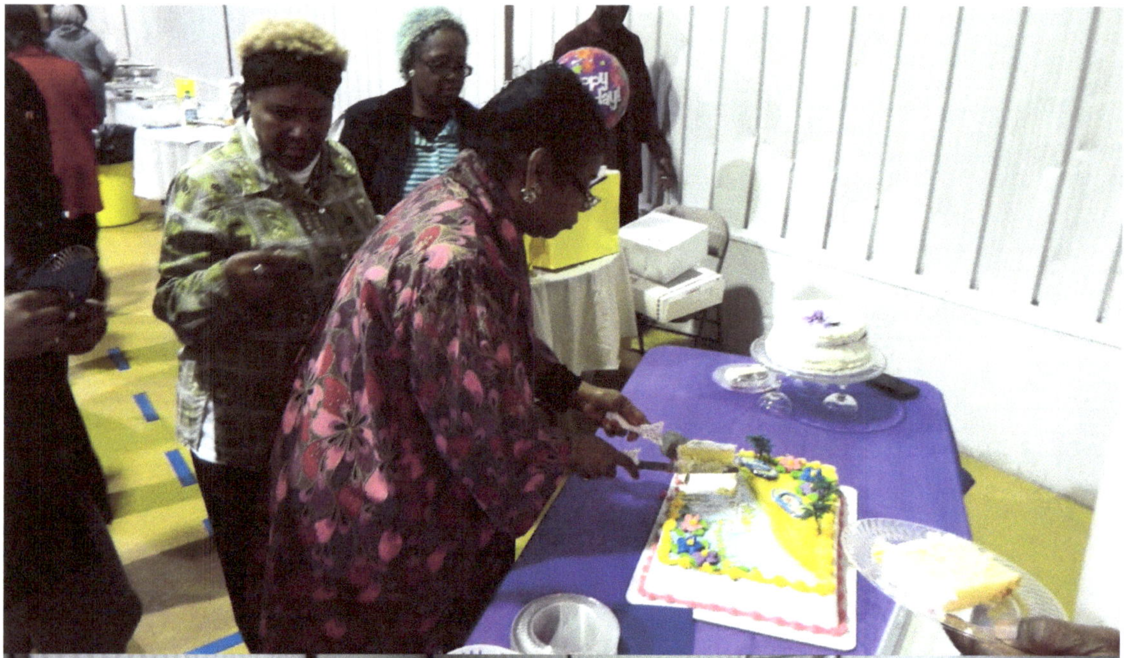

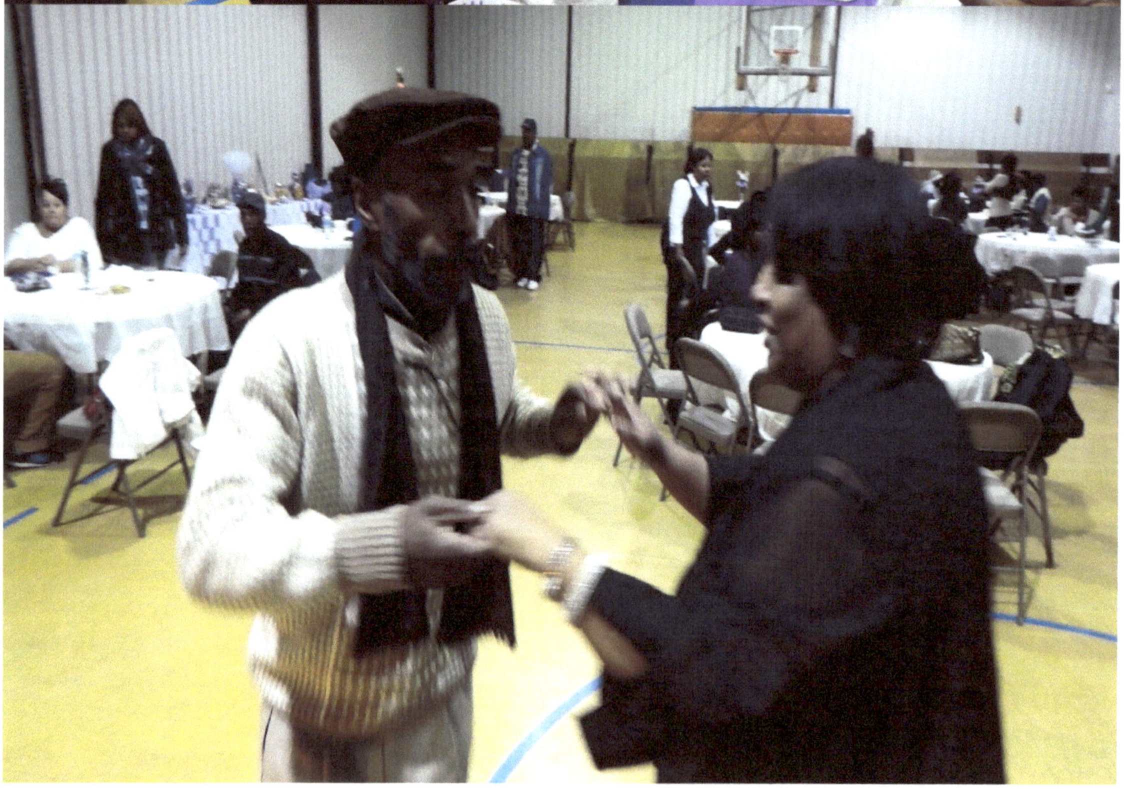

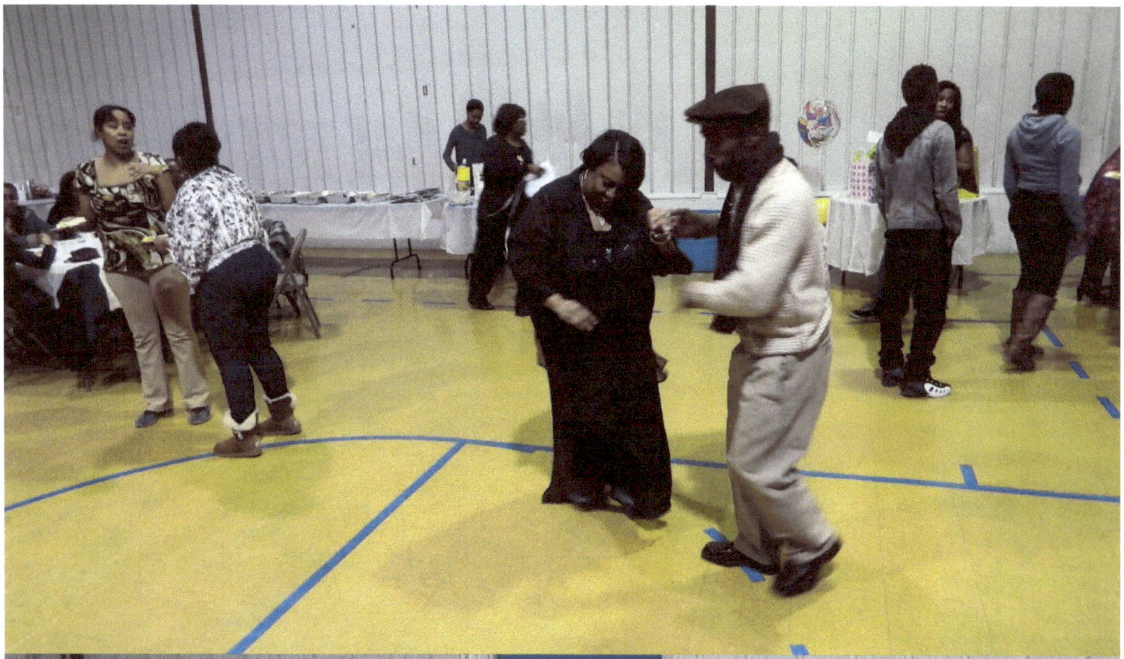

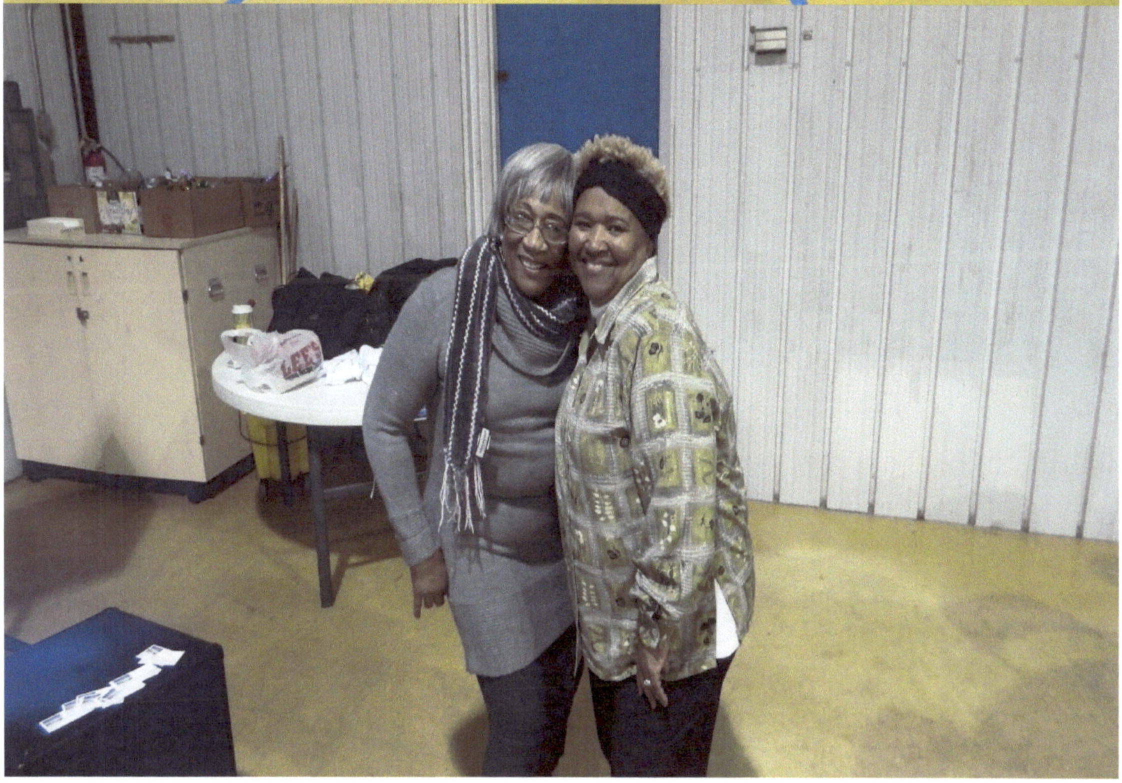

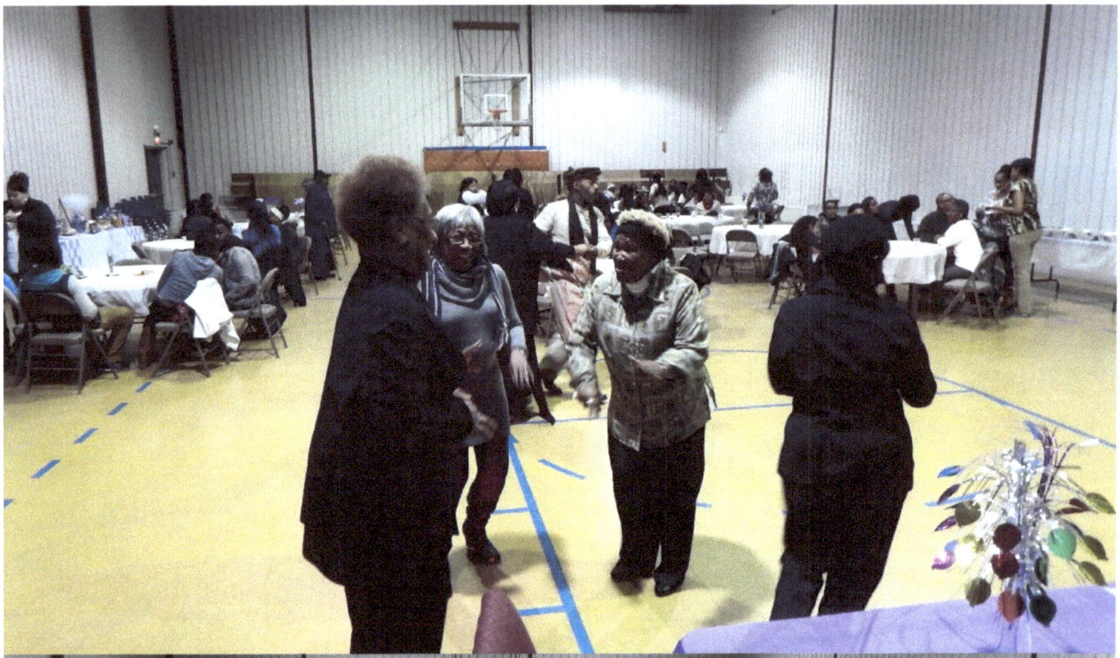

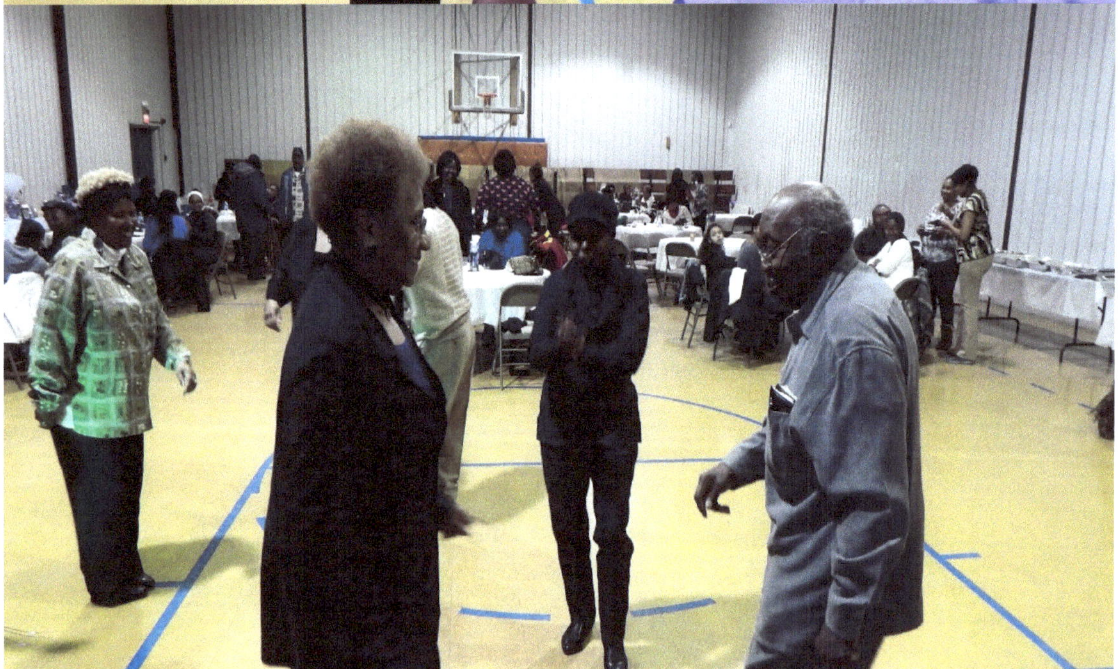

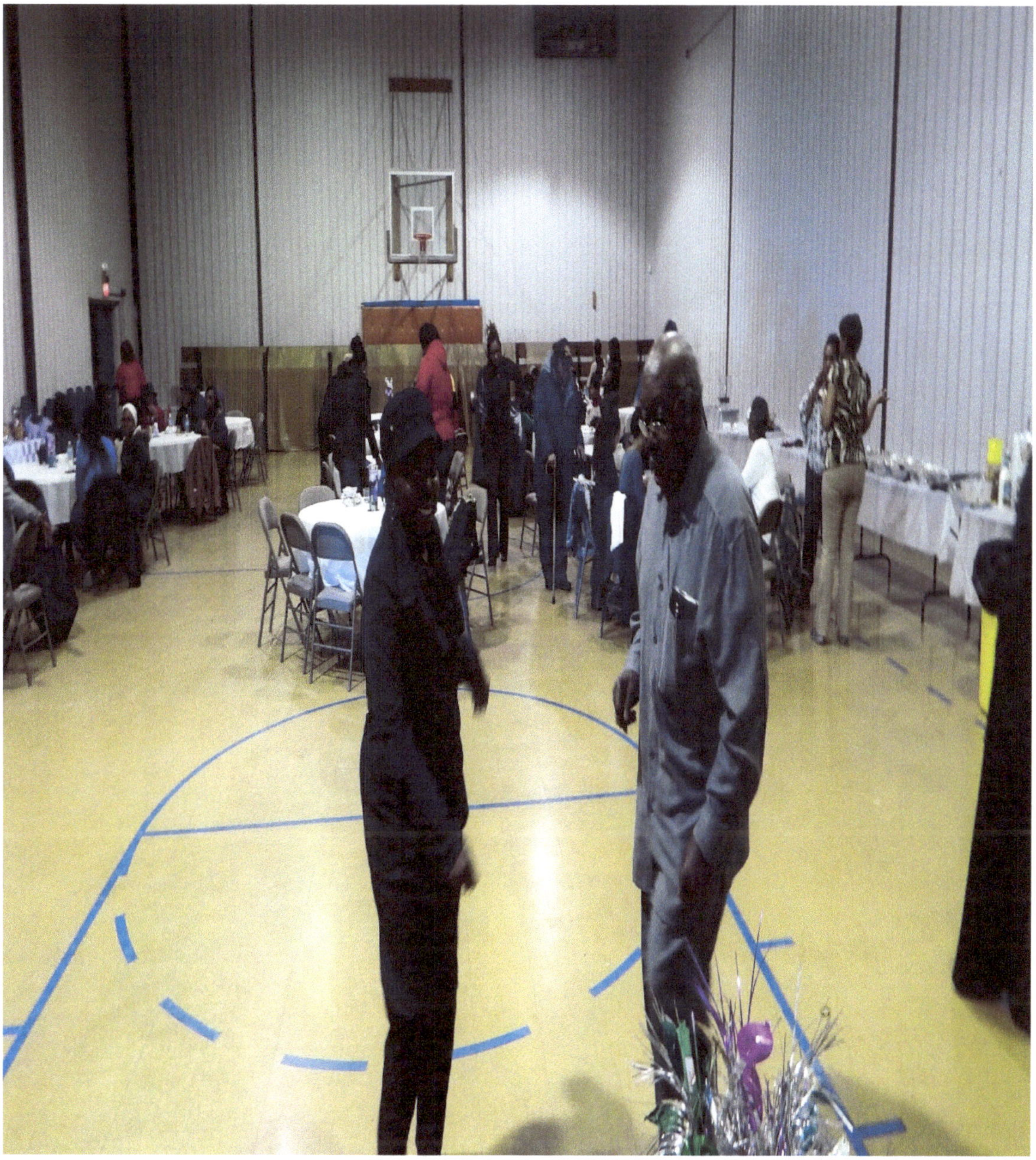

www.ingramcontent.com/pod-product-compliance
Lightning Source LLC
Chambersburg PA
CBHW050804180526
45159CB00004B/1546
9781507507421